SESE History Book 5
Helena Gannon

The Educational Company of Ireland

Note for Teachers and Parents

History Window On the World is a series of history books for third to sixth class. Using this series, children are encouraged to be active agents exploring the past. **History Window On the World** encourages them to be curious and excited about history while investigating and analysing primary sources. They work as historians, analysing primary sources such as documentary, pictorial, artefactual and oral evidence.

History Window On the World is in line with the Revised Curriculum and contains the appropriate strands and strand units for each class level. Children acquire the necessary knowledge and concepts while developing relevant skills and attitudes. **History Window On the World** allows for the investigation of personal, family and local history while learning about other significant historical topics.

History Window On the World allows children to learn in a fun and exciting way. They will develop an understanding of attitudes, beliefs and motivations of people in the past and gain a better insight into our world today. The development of historical skills encourages children to view situations from other people's perspectives.

Assessment is a key component of the **History Window On the World** series. There are four elements of assessment:

- **Question Time** uses lower and higher order questions to assess children's understanding of information while helping to develop higher order thinking skills.
- **Creative Time** stimulates children's imagination while also allowing children to develop empathy with characters from the past and explore history on another level through poetry, drama, music or art.
- **Puzzle Time** provides fun activities for reinforcing information.
- **Time Detective** enables children to develop skills while actively exploring the past.

The use of IT skills is catered for in the series with website references for teachers, parents and children to investigate. **Web Watch!** indicates a link to further information and page 111 contains **Web References** for each chapter in the book. Guided by the teacher or parent, children can explore each topic in greater detail and develop the skills of an historian in a fun and informative way.

Each chapter ends with a page dedicated to integration which is central to the Revised Curriculum. The teacher and pupils are provided with a wide array of ideas for integrating the topic into other subject areas, reinforcing the knowledge learned. A comprehensive Teacher's Resource Book is also available, with extra activities, ICT suggestions and photocopiable material.

We hope that children will enjoy using **History Window On the World** and that the skills of being an historian will give them pleasure and a life-long treasure.

Helena Gannon

Contents

Chapter	Topic	Strand	Strand Unit	Page
1	Buildings and Ruins in my Area	Local studies	Buildings, sites or ruins in my locality	4
2	Let's Communicate!	Continuity and change over time	Communications	10
3	Explorers Over Time	Continuity and change over time	Explorers	18
4	The Aztecs	Early people and ancient societies	Central and South American peoples	27
5	The Kingdom of Benin	Early people and ancient societies	African peoples	34
6	Revolution and Change	Politics, conflict and society	Revolution and change in America, France and Ireland	41
7	An Gorta Mór	Eras of change and conflict	The Great Famine	50
8	Irish Cultural Revival	Life, society, work and culture in the past	Language and culture in late 19th and early 20th century Ireland	60
9	Easter Rising 1916	Politics, conflict and society	1916 and the foundation of the State	67
10	Let's Celebrate!	Local studies	Feasts and festivals in the past	77
11	Rosa Parks	Story	Stories from the lives of people in the past	85
12	Martin Luther King	Story	Stories from the lives of people in the past	92
13	Women Who Dare!	Eras of change and conflict	Changing roles of women in the 19th and 20th centuries	100
14	Quiz Time	Revision		108
15	Web References	Research	Project work	111
16	Timeline	Working as an historian		112

Placenames

Let us examine the history of your area. Every locality has its own history. You must look carefully for clues that tell us about the past. Sometimes, the name of a locality can provide information about what a place was like.

Many placenames begin with **Bally** or **Ballin**. These come from the Irish word *Baile*, which means town. Example: Ballina.

Placenames beginning with **Cill** or **Kill** tell us that there may have been a church there long ago. Kill can also mean wood. Example: Kilkenny.

Many towns and villages were built next to a shallow part of a river. A ford is a crossing place in a river. Example: Athlone.

Dun, **Don** or **Doon** in a placename tell us that there was once a fort built in the area. Example: Dundalk.

Many placenames begin with **Carrick** or **Carraig**, which means rock. They may have been built near or on a large rock. Example: Carrickmacross.

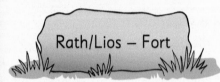

Many placenames use **Lis** or **Rath** in their names. These were forts built with earthen walls. Example: Lismore.

Other placenames begin with:
- **Ard** – high, tall
- **Mullagh/Mullach** – top, top of hill or mountain
- **Glenn/Glen** – valley

Make a list of placenames in your area which begin with these words. Try to find out what these placenames mean.

Web Watch!

http://www.irishtimes.com/ancestor/placenames/
http://goireland.about.com/od/historyculture/qt/irishplacenames.htm

Children work as historians, actively exploring buildings, sites and ruins in their locality.

Local Buildings or Ruins

Are there historic buildings or ruins in your area? Old buildings and ruins give us an idea about what life was like in the past. They help us to find out about the people who lived in our locality before us. Choose an old building in your area to research further.

Where to get information?

- Local library
- Internet
- Local people
- School library
- Local newspapers
- Old plaques
- Local historical societies

Some questions to help you get started:

- What is the oldest building in your locality?
- What is the building used for now?
- When was the building built?
- What materials were used in building it?
- Why was it built?
- What was the building used for?
- Did anyone ever live there?
- Does the building have a name?
- Was the building ever restored? Why?
- How has the building changed over the years?
- How has the building stayed the same?

What to look for

- Old photographs
- Old maps
- Old newspaper articles
- Information from older people

Plans

Draw plans for the old building.

- What, do you think, did it look like in the past?
- How many rooms were there?
- How many windows were there?
- Where were the entrances?
- What was the area of the building?

Poster Project

You could present your project as a poster project. Use a large poster page to present your work. Include lots of old photographs or drawings of what the building looked like in the past and how it looks now.

Peacock House

History

Plan of the House

Who Lived There

House in 1901

House Today

Question Time

1 What is the oldest building in your locality?
2 When was it built?
3 How could this old building or ruin be protected?
4 What does a placename containing 'Rath' tell you?
5 What does a placename beginning with 'Bally' or 'Ballin' tell you?
6 What is a shallow crossing in a river called?
7 Find out more about the name of the place in which you live.

Creative Time

1 Create a local heritage booklet for your area. The booklet could contain information about historic sites in your area. Include a map of the area with each of the historic sites clearly marked in. Your booklet would be a very useful resource for visitors and local historians.

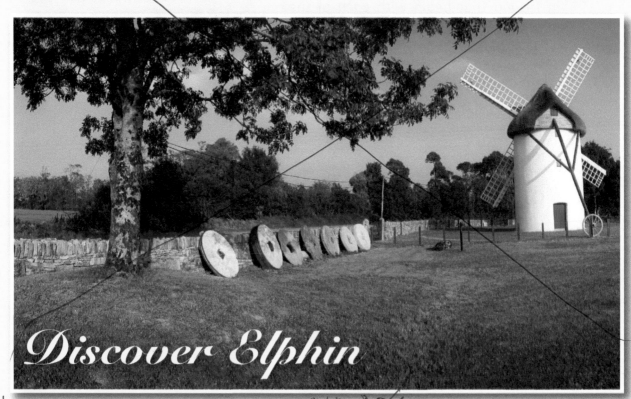

Discover Elphin

2 Draw a picture of what you think the inside of the building might have looked like when it was first built.
3 Write a song about your locality. You could choose a popular song and rewrite the lyrics. Remember to include local historic sites.

Puzzle Time

What, do you think, do the following placenames mean?

1 Kilkenny _____
2 Kildare _____
3 Carrickfergus _____
4 Dungarvan _____
5 Ballymore _____
6 Athlone _____
7 Rathdrum _____
8 Lismore _____
9 Dún Laoghaire _____
10 Ballinasloe _____

Time Detective

Using an atlas, write names of places in Ireland that begin with each of the following names. Mark them in on a map of Ireland.

■ Baile/Bally/Ballin

■ Rath/Lios

■ Carraig/Carrick

■ Dún/Doon/Don

■ Cill/Kill

■ Áth

■ Ard

■ Mullagh

■ Glen

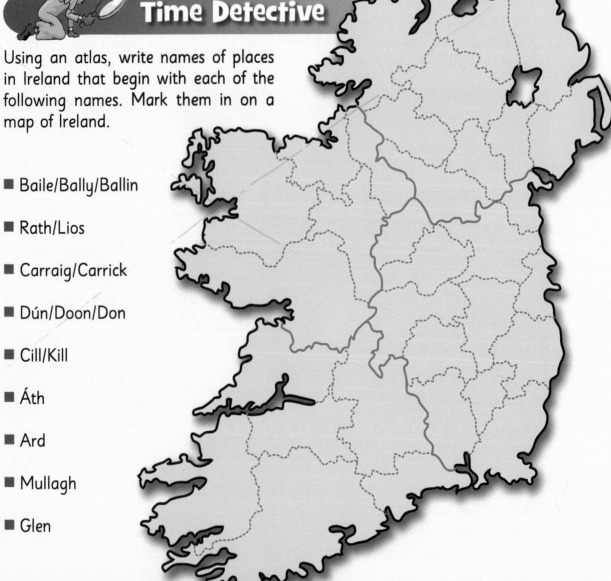

Integration Project

Buildings and Ruins in my Area

English

Write an acrostic poem about your local area. Each line of the poem begins with a letter from your placename.

Include things that are important or special to your area.

Gaeilge

Déan cairt de d'áit féin. Cuir isteach ainmneacha na sráideanna i nGaeilge.

Déan cur síos ar an gcaoi a bhfuair siad na hainmneacha sin.

Mathematics

Estimate the height of a tall building in your locality. Measure the length of the shadow it casts. Measure your own shadow. Divide the building's shadow by your shadow and multiply by your height.
This will tell you how tall the building is.

Drama

Choose an old building in your locality. Imagine that you are a family living or working there.

In small groups, act out a scene that might have taken place there in the past.

Geography

Draw a map of your locality. Mark in five places that are important to you. Use colours to show the different land uses such as green space, housing and shops. Mark in physical features in your area. Use a key.

SPHE

Investigate what food produce can be bought locally. Look at ways to reduce your food kilometres by buying local produce.

Make a list of local services and the food they produce.

Art

Design a crest or a badge for a local club in your area.

What images would be relevant and important to your locality?

Science

Working in groups, design and build a tall building using blocks.

What makes your building stronger?

Who can design and build the tallest building in the class?

What made their construction stronger?

2 | Let's Communicate!

People like to share ideas, thoughts or information with each other. There are many ways to communicate. We communicate by talking, telling stories, writing, emailing and sending text messages.

Today, technology plays a big part in how we communicate.

Fast Facts!

- Stone Age people drew paintings on the walls of caves to tell stories about hunting or battles.
- Smoke signals were used by Native Americans to send messages from one tribe to another.
- Drums were used on battlefields to direct the soldiers.
- Flags were used by sailors so that the crew of one ship could talk to another.
- 'Semaphore' is the system of signalling by human or mechanical arms.

Make a list of different methods of communication. Use the pictures to help you. Compare your list with those of your classmates. What is your favourite method of communication?

Inventors' Hall of Fame

Samuel Morse (1791-1872)

Samuel Morse was an American painter who invented Morse code in 1837. He proved that signals could be transmitted by wire. A system of dots and dashes was used to spell out words. The signals were translated by an operator.

Alexander Graham Bell (1847-1922)

Alexander Graham Bell, a Scottish scientist, invented the telephone in Boston in 1876. The first telephone conversation was to his assistant: 'Mr. Watson, come here, I want to see you.'

Guglielmo Marconi (1874-1937)

Marconi was an Irish-Italian inventor. He sent and received his first radio signal in 1895. In 1995, An Post released a postage stamp in his honour.

John Logie Baird (1888-1946)

John Logie Baird was a Scottish engineer who invented the first working television. The first human face was televised in 1925. He demonstrated the world's first colour transmission in July 1928.

Telephones over Time

Study the three telephones carefully and answer the following questions:

1 How does each telephone work?
2 What are the differences between each telephone?
3 What are the advantages or disadvantages of each telephone?
4 Which telephone would you like to use? Give reasons for your answer.

Radios over Time

Study the three radios carefully and answer the following questions:

1 How, do you think, do these radios work?
2 What changes have been made to the radio over the years?
3 How do we listen to the radio today?

Modern Communication

Over the years, technology has changed the way that we talk to each other. Satellites were sent into space and they helped to bounce radio signals all around the world. The first computers were developed in the 1940s. They were so big that only one computer could fit in a room!

Since then, computers have become smaller and smaller in size. They have also become much cheaper.

The Internet is a worldwide computer network. It was developed in the late 1960s. At first, very few people had the Internet. Later, more and more people began to use it. In the 1990s, the Internet became available to anyone with a computer. It can now be used on mobile phones as well.

We can surf the World Wide Web and gather information on almost any topic. It is like a great big library with millions of pages of information. Using the Internet, electronic messages, called emails, can be sent to anywhere in the world.

Question Time

1 How did people communicate in the past?
2 List some of the ways we communicate today.
3 Who invented Morse code?
4 What did John Logie Baird invent?
5 What was the first telephone conversation?
6 Which inventor was honoured with an Irish postal stamp in 1995?
7 What does 'www' stand for?
8 What is the Internet?
9 What are the benefits of the Internet?
10 What are the disadvantages of the Internet?

Creative Time

1 Working in small groups of four or five, choose one invention you have learned about. Imagine that you were trying to sell that invention today.

■ Create your own advertising campaign for your product.

■ How will you advertise it?

■ Design your own posters, television advertisement and catchy jingle to help sell your invention.

■ You want to convince people to buy your invention.
Present your campaign to your class.

2 Imagine that it is the year 2050. Design a method of communication used in this year. Draw your design and label it. Explain how it works.

Puzzle Time

Morse Code

A	.−	N	−.	0	−−−−−
B	−...	O	−−−	1	.−−−−
C	−.−.	P	.−−.	2	..−−−
D	−..	Q	−−.−	3	...−−
E	.	R	.−.	4	....−
F	..−.	S	...	5	.....
G	−−.	T	−	6	−....
H	....	U	..−	7	−−...
I	..	V	...−	8	−−−..
J	.−−−	W	.−−	9	−−−−.
K	−.−	X	−..−	.	.−.−.−
L	.−..	Y	−.−−	,	−−..−−
M	−−	Z	−−..	?	..−−..

1 Morse Code

Imagine that you are a telegraph operator. Find the words that are written in Morse code.

1 .... . .−.. .−.. −−−
HELLO

2 .... . .−.. .−−.
HELP

3 .. −. ...− . −. − −−− .−.
INVENTOR

4 −− . ...− −−. . ...
MESSAGES

5 −− −−− .−. ... .
MORSE

2 Sign Language

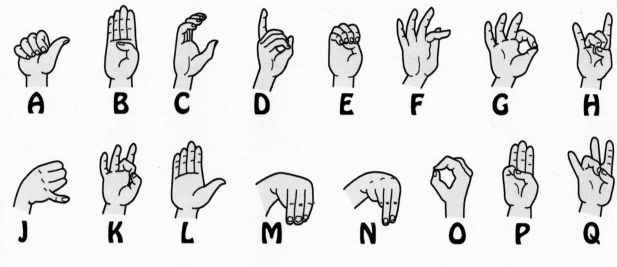

A B C D E F G H I

J K L M N O P Q R

S T U V W X Y Z

Sign a message to your friends. See if they can understand your message.

Time Detective

Working as an historian, investigate methods of communication in the past. Interview your parents, grandparents or elderly neighbours about how they communicated when they were young. Try to ask questions that will encourage people to think about their past. Write down their answers and present your information to the class in a project. Here are some sample questions to get you started:

- How did you communicate with your family and friends when you were young?
- How did you communicate with people who lived far away?
- What was the most popular way of communicating?
- Did you have a telephone? Describe it.
- Was there a computer in your house?

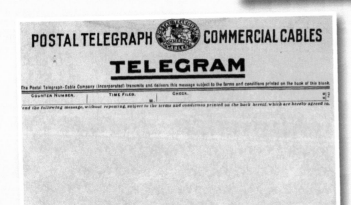

Web Watch!

http://www.battleshipnc.com/kids/games/morse/index.php

Integration Project

English

Working as a class, write your own radio broadcast. You could include songs, sport, music, school news, poems, stories and jokes.

Tape your broadcast and play it for other classes or transmit it over the school intercom.

Gaeilge

Scríobh script shimplí chun dráma a dhéanamh don teilifís. I ngrúpa beag bí ag aisteoireacht.

Mathematics

Estimate how many phone numbers are in your local telephone directory. How would you work it out? (Hint: How many numbers are in a column? How many on a page? How many pages for each letter?)

Drama

Working in pairs, investigate a famous inventor. Then act out an interview with this inventor including all the information you have learned.

Let's Communicate!

Geography

Choose a country you would like to visit some day. Investigate that country. Write a postcard from that country. Include information about the climate, places to visit and interesting facts.

Music

Working in groups, use different musical instruments to communicate different emotions.

Your classmates have to guess which emotions you are trying to communicate.

SPHE

How do you communicate without using spoken words?

Try to communicate a sentence to your partner using non-verbal ways.

What methods did you use?

Science

Investigate how telephones work. Create your own telephone using two paper cups and some string. Use a pencil to make a small hole in each of the paper cups. Pass one end of the string through each hole and tie a knot inside each cup. With a partner, try talking to each other using your string telephone.

Since the beginning of time, people have always wanted to explore the unknown. Early explorers set out to find trade routes, treasures, glory for their countries and sometimes to spread religion. Exploration is a way of learning about the world. Here are some of the famous explorers and their explorations.

James Cook (1728-1779)

Cook was a British explorer who explored the Pacific Ocean, Antarctic and Arctic. He was an expert cartographer (map maker).

Christopher Columbus (1451-1506)

Columbus sailed west across the Atlantic Ocean in search of Asia. Instead, he found land in the Caribbean Sea.

Amerigo Vespucci (1454-1512)

This Italian explorer realised that America was a different continent from Asia. America was named after him.

Hernán Cortés (1485-1547)

Cortés was a ruthless Spanish explorer who conquered and destroyed the Aztec empire of Mexico.

Francisco Pizarro (1478-1541)

Pizarro was a Spanish explorer who travelled to South America and conquered the Incas.

Children investigate explorers through the ages, studying one explorer in more detail.

Vasco Da Gama (1460-1524)

Da Gama was a Portuguese explorer who found an ocean route from Portugal to India around the Cape of Good Hope.

Marco Polo (1254-1324)

Marco Polo was an Italian explorer who travelled to China along the Silk Road. The journey took almost four years.

Ferdinand Magellan (1480-1521)

This Portuguese explorer led the first expedition that sailed around the world. Unfortunately, he died before completing the journey.

Abel Tasman (1603-1659)

The Dutchman Abel Tasman discovered New Zealand and Fiji. However, he sailed around Australia without realising that it was there!

Roald Amundsen (1872-1928)

Amundsen was a Norwegian polar explorer. He was the first person to reach the South Pole, in 1911.

Word Watch!

Trade Routes were new and easier routes that explorers found to move goods from place to place.

19

Project Time

Choose one explorer and investigate his/her exploration in more detail.
Design a poster advertising for crew members to go on the exploration.

How will the explorer convince them to join the exploration?

Where?
Where did they explore?

How?
How did they get to their destination?

When?
When did the exploration take place?

Biography?
When was he/she born?
Where was he/she born?

Explorer: Who?

Legacy?
What are they famous for?

Map
Draw a map of their exploration.

Why?
Why did they choose this destination?

What?
What happened on the exploration?
Tell their story.

Irish Explorers

Brendan the Navigator

St Brendan was known as 'Brendan the Navigator'. He was born in Co. Kerry in 484. He and his crew sailed west in a small boat called a currach. The journey took seven years. He is thought to have also travelled to Scotland and possibly Iceland. Some believe that St Brendan even reached America. When he returned from his travels, he told great stories of his amazing adventures. St Brendan became the patron saint of sailors, travellers and whales!

Tom Crean (1877-1938)

Tom Crean was born in Co. Kerry in 1877. Tom joined the Royal Navy at the age of fifteen. In 1901, Captain Scott and his crew were on an expedition to explore the Antarctic. They chose Tom to join the crew. Tom placed the first ever Irish flag on the Antarctic. On his second expedition with Captain Scott, they raced to the South Pole. When they got closer to the South Pole, Scott chose four others to go with him. Crean was devastated not to be chosen. His third and final expedition to the South Pole was in 1914 under Sir Ernest Shackleton. Tom returned to Kerry in 1920 and opened a pub called the 'South Pole Inn'.

Pat Falvey

Pat Falvey was born in Cork in 1957. He is an adventurer and explorer. He climbed Mount Everest in 1995 and again in 2004. He is the only person in the world to have climbed the highest peak on each of the seven continents twice. In January 2008, he led the first Irish expedition to reach the South Pole. They retraced the steps of Tom Crean.

Did You Know?

The first explorers had to depend on their observations of the moon and stars to find their way. Ancient explorers thought the world was flat and feared falling off!

The Viking explorer Leif Eriksson left Greenland in 1001 to search for land to the southwest. He is believed to be officially the first European to have found North America. He called it Vinland.

The Spanish King Ferdinand and Queen Isabella funded Christopher Columbus's expedition. He set out with three ships, the *Nina*, the *Pinta* and the *Santa Maria*. He thought he had discovered China when he had in fact landed in America.

Roald Amundsen and Robert Scott were in a race to be the first explorer to reach the South Pole. Scott arrived one month after Amundsen to find the Norwegian flag. Unfortunately, Scott's team died of cold and hunger on their return trip.

New Zealander Edmund Hillary was the first person to successfully climb Mount Everest, the world's highest mountain peak, in 1953. He and his team could not stay long as they had to get back to camp before their oxygen ran out.

Irish explorer Dr Clare O'Leary from Co. Cork was the first Irish woman to climb Mount Everest. She was also the first Irish woman to reach the South Pole as part of Pat Falvey's team.

Loop Game

Divide your class into small groups of two. Each group in your class has a card. Listen to find out if your card is the correct answer. Then read out your card. You can start with any card.

| I have Christopher Columbus. | Who has the Portuguese explorer who led the first expedition to sail around the world? |

| I have Ferdinand Magellan. | Who has the Italian explorer who travelled to China? |

| I have Leif Eriksson. | Who has the Dutch explorer who discovered New Zealand and Fiji? |

| I have Vasco Da Gama. | Who has the Irish explorer who led an all-Irish expedition to the South Pole? |

| I have Francisco Pizarro. | Who has the first person to reach the South Pole? |

| I have Hernán Cortés. | Who has the British explorer who explored the Pacific Ocean, Arctic and Antarctic? |

| I have Pat Falvey. | Who has the Irish explorer who explored the Antarctic three times? |

| I have Tom Crean. | Who has the Irish saint known as Brendan the Voyager? |

| I have Saint Brendan. | Who has the Spanish explorer who conquered the Aztec empire? |

| I have Marco Polo. | Who has the leader of the Antarctic expedition in 1914? |

| I have Amerigo Vespucci. | Who has the Spanish explorer who conquered the Inca empire? |

| I have James Cook. | Who has the explorer who sailed west to discover a new route to Asia? |

| I have Roald Amundsen. | Who has the Viking explorer who is thought to be the first European to sail to America? |

| I have Abel Tasman. | Who has the explorer that was the first European to sail to India? |

| I have Ernest Shackleton. | Who has the first person to climb Mount Everest? |

| I have Edmund Hillary. | Who has the explorer that America was named after? |

Question Time

1 What are some of the reasons for exploration?
2 Name the explorer who officially first discovered America.
3 What dangers, do you think, might early explorers have faced?
4 Which explorer led the first expedition around the world?
5 Name the three ships Columbus used on his expedition.
6 Why, do you think, did King Ferdinand and Queen Isabella fund Columbus's expedition?
7 What country did Columbus think he had discovered by sailing west?
8 How, do you think, did Captain Scott select his four explorers for the final part of his expedition?
9 How many expeditions did Tom Crean undertake to the South Pole?
10 Who led the first Irish expedition to reach the South Pole?
11 Name the first Irish woman to reach the South Pole.
12 Who, do you think, is the greatest explorer? Give reasons for your choice.

Creative Time

1 Imagine that you are an explorer embarking on an exciting exploration. Choose one exploration you would like to undertake. Make a checklist of all the supplies you would need with you for your adventure.

2 You need money to fund this exploration. Write a letter to your country's leader asking for money to help fund your exploration. Tell the leader the reasons for your trip and explain how you would spend the money.

3 Make your own compass.
- **You will need:** magnet, paper clip, water, bowl, cork and compass.
- Fill the bowl with water. Place the cork floating in the water.
- Rub the paper clip with the magnet for several minutes in the same direction.
- Place the paper clip on top of the cork. The magnet will point to the north and south poles. Use a compass to check.

4 Frederick T. Bear has accompanied Irish explorer Pat Falvey and his team on their expeditions. Read the following extract from his diary as he climbs Mount Everest:

Sunday 18 May 2003

We have lots of work today – organising food, medicine and oxygen. We all put on our oxygen masks and regulators, as we need to make sure everything is working and fitted properly. The mask feels strange on my face when I try it on, and when I walk around; I can't even see my feet! Pat says we all have to go outside for a while, wearing all our gear, to try and get used to it. It's really cool. During the afternoon, everyone wants to call home to speak to their families before they leave for the summit and into a place called Death Zone.

Freddy

Imagine that you are on this expedition with Freddy and Pat Falvey. Write the next diary entry he might have written.

Puzzle Time

Who am I?

One member of the class sits on a chair at the top of the room. He/she becomes a famous explorer. Members of the class, in turn, ask the explorer questions. The explorer can only answer yes or no. After ten questions, the class must guess which explorer they are questioning!

Time Detective

Working as an historian, investigate space exploration. Who were some of the famous explorers who ventured into space? Create your own timeline.

Web Watch!

Find out more about Pat Falvey's adventures on: http://www.patfalvey.com and about Dr Clare O'Leary on http://www.southernstar.ie/article.php?id=507

Read more about Frederick T. Bear in this book: Freddy's Everest Diary: The Dream of Frederick T. Bear by Pat Falvey and Clare O'Leary, published by The Collins Press, 2004

http://www.theteacherscorner.net/thematicunits/explorers.htm
http://www.coreknowledge.org/CK/resrcs/lessons/06_5_EyeExplore.pdf
http://teachersnetwork.org/adaptors/taylsacr/explore.htm

Integration Project

English

Create your own Explorer Trading cards. Each person selects a different explorer. Create information cards about the explorer. Put in facts about that person's explorations such as dates, countries explored, and other information.

Gaeilge

Déan pas den taiscéalaí is fearr leat.
Déan pictiúr freisin.

Mathematics

Christopher Columbus's ship, the *Santa Maria*, was 18 metres in length. Measure out this length in the yard.
Are you surprised at its size? Can you find any other items that would be of similar length?

Oral language

Working in pairs, choose a favourite explorer. Each pair gives a speech to the class convincing them that their explorer is the best.

Hold a class election with each student voting for who he/she thinks is the best explorer.

Explorers Over Time

Geography

Plan your own expedition. What country would you like to explore?
What route will you take?
What method of transport will you use?
What obstacles will you face? Make a map of your journey.

IT

Create a PowerPoint presentation of your favourite explorer.
Include images and text about your explorer.
Present your slideshow to your class. For more information, visit:
http://www.enchantedlearning.com/explorers/

Art

A diorama is a miniature three-dimensional scene.

Create a class diorama of exploration.

You could use fabric, cardboard, clay, tissue and crepe paper to create your diorama.

Science

Early explorers brought back many new spices.

Can you identify several different spices just by using your sense of smell? Spices will be placed in a clear container.

Work as a group to try and name the correct spice.

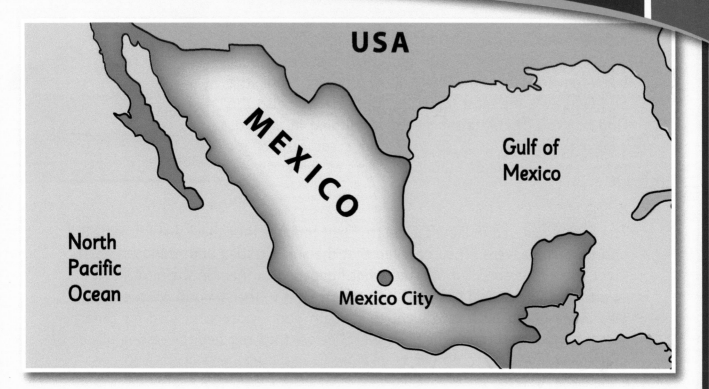

The Aztecs were a wandering people who left their home in Atzlan in North West Mexico in order to find new land. They searched for many years for somewhere to settle until their leader had a vision. He was told to search for a special sign – an eagle perched on a cactus eating a snake.

He led his people to a swampy land in the middle of Lake Texcoco. Here, in 1325, they built the city of Tenochtitlán. The great Aztec Empire had begun.

- Why, do you think, did the Aztecs build their city on a lake?
- What were the advantages?
- What were the disadvantages?

The Aztecs made islands by piling up plants and mud from the lake. These islands were called *chinampas*. Trees were planted to hold the soil together. They built mud huts and some small temples. Canoes were used to travel from the islands.

Today, the Mexican flag shows an eagle sitting on a cactus eating a snake.

Acamapichtli was chosen as their first Emperor. The city grew quickly. Over the years it became one of the largest cities in the world.

Children work as historians exploring the everyday lives of the Aztecs and examining evidence from this ancient society.

Religion

Religion was very important in Aztec life. The Aztecs worshipped hundreds of gods and goddesses. They built huge temples to honour their gods. Huitzilopochtli, the Sun God, was the most important god. He was also the God of War. The Aztecs believed everything in life was controlled by the gods so they had great respect for them. They even made human sacrifices to the gods.

Beliefs

The Aztecs believed in life after death. They thought that there were nine hells and thirteen heavens. They believed that the sun wrestled with darkness each night. How a person died affected what happened to them in the next life. If a soldier died on the field of battle, he went straight to the sun god. Women who died while giving birth also went to the sun god. Those who died for other reasons travelled through the underworld before they reached the resting place of the dead.

Warfare

The Aztecs often fought in battles with their neighbours. Warfare was an important part of everyday life for the Aztecs. The Aztec wealth grew as they conquered more land. Every boy was trained to fight. Boys learned about fighting and weapons in school. Fighting in battle was considered an honour. The Aztecs fought with spears, javelins, shields, slings, bows and arrows. Prisoners of war were used as sacrifices in religious ceremonies.

Aztec Justice

The Aztecs had very harsh punishments for those who committed crimes. Criminals were taken to court where a group of judges decided their fate.

Crime	Punishment
Cutting down a living tree	Death
Drunkenness (1st offence)	Head shaved and house destroyed
Drunkenness (2nd offence)	Death
Major theft	Death
Minor theft	Sold into slavery

Daily Life

Most Aztecs were farmers. They grew fruit and vegetables on their swampy land. Their main food was maize, a type of corn. They also hunted and fished for food. Food was cooked on a hearth. The Aztecs made their own clothes. Women wore skirts, while men wore a poncho or cloak with a loincloth underneath. The Aztecs sold maize and cotton in markets.

They loved to play the ball game *Tlachtli*. This game was a mix of modern football and basketball. Two teams played against each other. The aim was to hit the ball into a hoop using their knees. The Aztecs were also excellent stoneworkers, scribes and potters.

Cortés Lands

Hernán Cortés, the Spanish explorer, landed in the Aztec Empire in 1519. He had a group of about 600 soldiers with him. The Spanish army was armed with guns and cannons. Cortés burned every one of his ships to make sure that his troops could not retreat. The Aztecs welcomed him thinking he was a messenger from the Gods. He was given gifts of food, jewels and gold.

Cortés then set out with his army for Tenochtitlán. Along his travels, he invited enemies of the Aztecs to join him. In November 1519, Cortés and his men reached the Aztec capital. The Aztec Emperor, Moctezuma II, treated Cortés and his soldiers well. He may have thought that Cortés was a god-king.

However, Cortés was afraid that the Aztecs might soon try to get rid of him, so he took Moctezuma hostage. In June 1520, the Aztecs drove Cortés and his army out of their city. Cortés did not give up easily. He gathered up his army again and, in the summer of 1521, he returned and this time he captured Tenochtitlán.

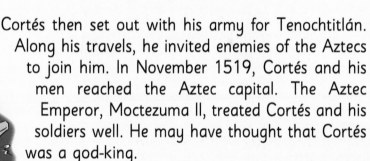

Many Aztecs were killed and thousands more died from smallpox, a disease which had been carried over by the Spanish soldiers. After the fighting was over, the city was destroyed. The Aztec Empire had come to an end. Later, the city of Mexico was built on the ruins of Tenochtitlán.

Let's Dig!

1 Divide your class into small groups of three. Each group draws a site map. Photographs of artefacts can be buried in a box filled with soil. Then, the groups go on an archaeological dig. Each member of the group has a different role:

(a) **Dig Excavator:** Uncovers the artefact, marks where the artefact was discovered on the site map.

(b) **Dig Secretary:** Sketches the artefact, noting the details, and marks where the artefact was discovered.

(c) **Archaeologist:** Examines the artefact and decides what it might have been used for.

2 Imagine that you have made an amazing archaeological discovery, uncovering remains of the Aztec empire. Study the following artefacts carefully and write up a group report on your findings. Remember to include a site map marking where the artefacts were discovered, detailed sketches of each artefact and your opinion about them.

Question Time

1 Where did the Aztecs come from originally?
2 Why did they build their city in the middle of a lake?
3 Who was the first emperor of the Aztecs?
4 What were *chinampas*?
5 How did the Aztecs travel between the islands?
6 Name the most important Aztec god.
7 What food did the Aztecs eat?
8 What games did the Aztecs play?
9 Why, do you think, did Cortés have every one of his ships burned?
10 Why, do you think, were the Aztecs beaten by a small Spanish army?

Creative Time

1 Create your own brochure encouraging people to travel to the city of Tenochtitlán. Include pictures of what you think the city looks like and why people should choose to visit this Aztec city.

2 Imagine that you are the Aztecs meeting Hernán Cortés for the first time. Organise a group meeting to discuss what you think you should do.

- How should he be treated?
- Should he be welcomed into your community?
- Is he a god?
- What might happen if you welcome him to stay in your community?

Each group forms a different opinion and tries to convince the group of their decision.

3 The Aztecs wrote in pictures called glyphs instead of words. Design your own Aztec glyphs.

Remember, they had their own rules for drawing. The head and feet were always shown from the side, while the body was shown from the front.

 grass
 house
 rabbit
 flower
 death
 dog
 rain
 flint
 eagle

Puzzle Time

Fill in the blanks:

The Aztecs came from ___ALSAN___ in North West Mexico. They left in search of a new home. The most important God to the Aztecs was ___HEIZEONO___. He was the God of ___MAIZE___. Islands in the lakes were called ___CHINAMPAS___. The Aztecs travelled between these islands in ___CANOOS___. They built huge ___TEMPLES___ to honour their gods. Warfare was an important part of Aztec life. Boys learned about fighting and weapons in ___SCHOOL___. Prisoners of war were used as ___SALRQAPCES___ in religious ceremonies. The Spanish explorer ___HERNAN CORTES___ landed in 1519. He destroyed the city of ___TENOCHTPTLAN___ and built Mexico City on its ruins.

Time Detective

Using your encyclopaedia or the Internet, create a timeline showing the important dates and events in the history of Mexico. Here are some dates and events to get you started:

- **1100** The Aztecs left their homeland in search of new home.

- **1325** The city of Tenochtitlán was founded.

- **1519** Hernán Cortés arrives in Mexico.

Web Watch!

http://www.innovationslearning.co.uk/subjects/history/information/aztecs/aztecs_home.htm
http://library.thinkquest.org/4034/cortes.html
http://www.azteccalendar.com/
http://www.teachnet-lab.org/miami/2003/mgil2.htm

Integration Project

English

Stories were told by the Aztecs to explain their beliefs and customs. Read some Aztec myths and legends to learn about their lives and to develop an understanding of their culture.

Gaeilge

Tá tú ag taisteal ar an mbád leis an taiscéalaí Hernán Cortés.
Scríobh i ndialann faoin turas.
Luaigh na smaointe atá agat, an faitíos agus an dóchas atá ort.

Mathematics

The Aztecs had two calendars. One had 365 days. The year was divided into eighteen months, each with twenty days. There were five unlucky days. The other calendar had 260 days, divided into twenty thirteen-day weeks. To find out more about the Aztec calendars, visit: http://www.azteccalendar.com/calendar-calculator.html

Drama

Hot Seat: One member of the class takes on the role of Hernán Cortés and sits in the 'Hot Seat'.

Take it in turns to ask him questions about his encounters with the Aztecs.

The Aztecs

Geography

Investigate Mexico today. Write **five** things you would like to know about the country. Research and find the answers to your questions. Share your information with your class.

Physical Education

Play the Aztec ball game *Tlachtli*.

The game is like basketball but you cannot use your hands.

Try shooting the ball into the hoop using only your knees.

Art

Use *papier maché* or a paper plate to make your own Aztec mask.

Your mask could be in honour of the sun god.

Science

The sun was very sacred to the Aztecs. They had ceremonies to celebrate the sun.

Make a fact sheet about the sun and investigate solar energy. To read about making your own solar oven, visit:
http://www.solarnow.org/pizzabx.htm

The Kingdom of Benin is located in modern day Southern Nigeria, Africa. It became very powerful between 1200 and 1300 AD. The Kingdom grew as new farms and villages were built. Most people made their living from farming. Yams were their main food.

Benin City was the capital of the Kingdom. For over 600 years, it was the centre of a rich, well-organised empire. The city was surrounded by large earth walls to protect it from attack.

The people of Benin were known as 'Edo'. They spoke a language also called Edo. They were famous in Africa as warriors, traders and skilled metalworkers.

Word Watch!
A **Yam** is a large vegetable like a sweet potato

Children investigate the ancient Kingdom of Benin and become familiar with aspects of the lives of the people who lived there.

'The town is composed of thirty main streets, very straight and thirty metres wide, apart from an infinity of small intersecting streets... The houses... have roofs, verandahs and balustrades, and are covered with leaves of palm-trees and bananas – for they are only one storey high... in the houses of gentlemen there are long galleries within and many rooms whose walls and floors are of red earth. These people... wash and scrub their houses so well that they are polished and shining like glass.'

Samuel Blomert, Dutch Traveller, 17th century

During the 15th century, Portuguese explorers began to travel to West Africa and trade with the people of Benin. The King of Benin allowed the Portuguese to set up a trading station. The Portuguese traded gums, oils, black pepper and ivory in exchange for fabrics, copper and beads.

The artists of Benin were very talented and skilled and produced some of the most wonderful art in Africa. Many of the craftspeople of Benin were organised into groups or guilds. Each guild lived in its own part of the city called wards. Women were not allowed to join the guilds. The Kingdom of Benin grew in wealth as a result of this international trade.

Bronze pieces from the Kingdom of Benin are famous all over the world. Almost all their art was created to honour the king, or Oba.

The Oba's Palace

'The people of Benin worship the sun, and believe that spirits are immortal, and that after death they go to the sun... When the king dies, the people all assemble in a large field, in the centre of which is a very deep well... They cast the body of the dead king into this well and those who are judged to have been most dear to and favoured by the king... go down to keep him company. When they have done so, the people place a great stone over the well and remain by it day and night.'

Portuguese sailor's account, 16th century

The Kingdom of Benin was ruled by the all-powerful king called an Oba. The people believed the king was a God. Everyone had to obey the Oba. His huge palace was decorated with bronze statues and wood carvings. The palace was laid out in courtyards. There were separate areas for the Oba, his wives and children and palace officials. The entrance gate has a tall tower with a huge brass snake on top. A special shrine was made in honour of the king and sacrifices were made there.

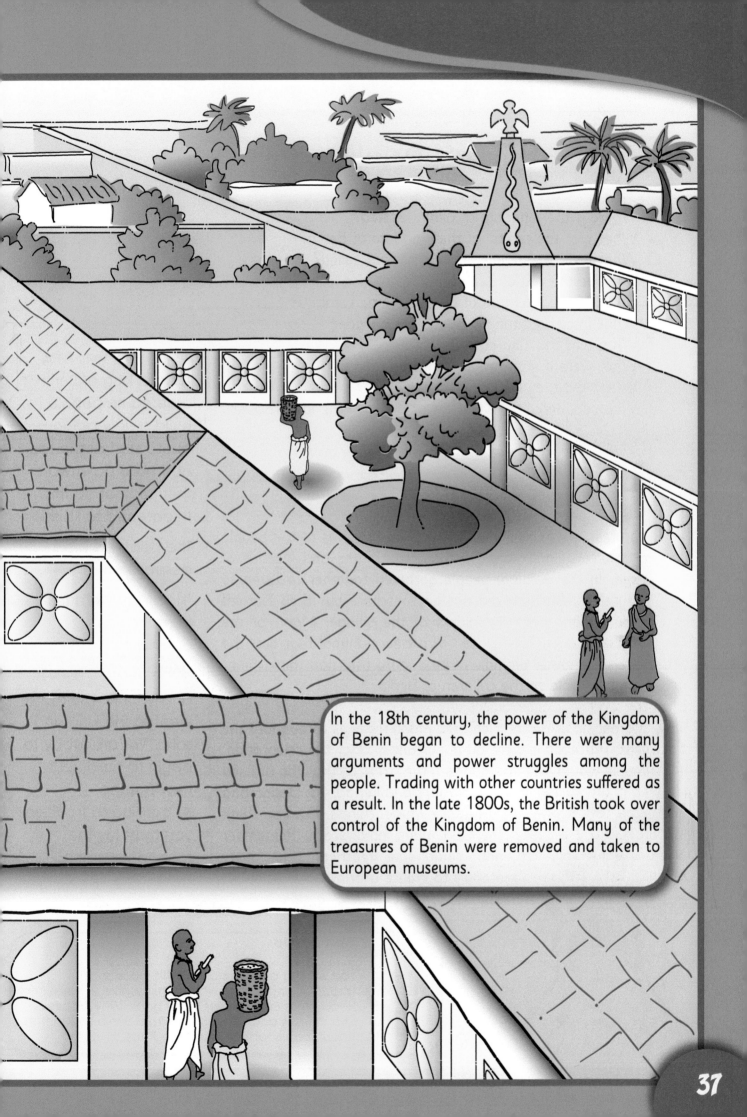

In the 18th century, the power of the Kingdom of Benin began to decline. There were many arguments and power struggles among the people. Trading with other countries suffered as a result. In the late 1800s, the British took over control of the Kingdom of Benin. Many of the treasures of Benin were removed and taken to European museums.

Question Time

1 Where is the Kingdom of Benin located?
2 What was the capital of the Kingdom of Benin?
3 What were the people of the Kingdom called?
4 Describe the city of Benin.
5 How did the Kingdom of Benin become wealthy?
6 What goods did the people of Benin trade?
7 What was the king called?
8 What were a group of craftspeople called?
9 Where did they live?
10 Who conquered the Kingdom of Benin in the late 1800s?

Creative Time

1 Storytelling was an important part of the lives of the people of Benin. Children learned about the myths and legends of Benin. In the evening, people gathered together to listen to storytellers. Children did not go to school but they learned many lessons from the elders of the village. Many of the stories tell about a 'trickster' or a clever animal that gets the better of another animal. Write a story that you think might have been told to the children of Benin.

2 The people of Benin celebrated many festivals throughout the year. Processions were an important part of the celebration. People would sing and dance in the street as the Oba dressed in ceremonial robes and headdress. Design and make your own headdress that you think the Oba might have worn. Remember you could use feathers and other materials to create a bright and colourful headdress suitable for a king.

A short story from Benin

A cruel king of Benin ordered his people to build a new palace but to start at the top and build downward. If they did not do this, he threatened to kill them.

The people were in despair.

'How can we build from the top downward?' they asked.

Finally, one wise man went to the king and said: 'We are ready to begin to build your new palace. According to tradition, you must lay the foundation stone!'

Web Watch!

You will find a Benin story on this website:
http://justjungle.com/why_monkeys_live_in_trees.html
Read other Benin stories in this book: Why Monkeys Live in Trees and Other Stories from Benin by Mama Raouf, published by Curbstone Press.

Puzzle Time

Find the following words in the wordsearch.

- bronze
- craftspeople
- Edo
- guilds
- ivory
- metalworkers
- Oba
- Portuguese
- procession
- shrine
- traders
- wards

```
T R A D E R S D L I U G K V K
L U C H J H F I K Q T V F Z R
D E V B W H D P V Q H C Z S R
V S D R A W I T S O V C W M R
Q E M B S L F Q B S R S M E P
V U O N F O X R D A L Y T K S
I G W A O B O N F X V E M R L
A U R E H N N T K V N N W O F
O T N F Z X S A V C A I A W O
D R Q E C P N A Z D S R Y L A
E O G Z E P T Y I K P H N A G
N P R O C E S S I O N S T T U
U D P T A V M X U B P V K E I
C L T N W A F I V U L Q P M X
E U W K E V V Y G C J Y Y X B
```

Time Detective

Working as an historian, imagine that you are walking through the city of Benin. Write about the sights, smells, sounds and tastes that you experience. After passing through the gate in the city walls, visit the wards of the city, the market and the Oba's palace.

Web Watch!

http://africa.mrdonn.org/benin.html
http://www.uiowa.edu/~africart/
http://www.dia.org/collections/aonwc/africanart/beninkings.html
http://www.smb.spk-berlin.de/mv/afrika/e/koenig1.htm
http://www.nmafa.si.edu/exhibits/beninfr.htm
http://www.dia.org/collections/aonwc/africanart/72.435.html

Integration Project

English

Read the ancient story of Ogun and Emotan. This tale is a story told by the people of Benin about their ancestors and their history. It is available in the Teacher's Resource Book.

Gaeilge

Déan póstaer 'Wanted' ag lorg duine atá ag gearán agus ag cur isteach ar an Oba. Tarraing an duine agus cuir isteach an fáth a bhfuil an Oba á lorg.

Mathematics

Traders in Benin did not use coins. They bartered goods (exchanged goods) or used cowrie shells or manillas (Portuguese bracelets) as currency. Using counters, act out a market scene where counters are used in exchange for goods.

The Kingdom of Benin

Drama

Recreate Benin City market in your classroom. Each member of your class takes on a different role. Traders sell leather belts, tunics, wooden cups, bowls and food. Others sell animals such as monkeys and parrots. Wealthy traders sell glass, fabric and beads.

Geography

Investigate the African country Nigeria.
The location of the Kingdom of Benin was in south central Nigeria, east of Lagos.
Write a traveller's guide to visiting Benin.

Music

Working in small groups, create your own chant that might have been sung during the Oba's procession through the palace.
Sing your chant for the class.

Art

Examine the art of Benin. Examine the brass plaques that were used to show the power of the king. Create your own wall plaque showing power and authority. Visit:
http://www.nmafa.si.edu/exhibits/benintwo.htm

Science

Make a poster about the animals that lived in the ancient Kingdom of Benin. Animals such as monkeys, parrots, eagles, leopards, chickens, antelopes, bush-rats, red wart-hogs, crocodiles, snakes, scorpions and cane rats all lived there.

The late 18th century was a period of unrest and change. People began to demand more freedom and control in their own countries.

The American Revolution

From the 1600s, British colonists sailed to America to settle. Britain ruled thirteen colonies there. After the Seven Years War (1756–1763) between Britain and France for control of North America, Britain decided to bring in taxes making the colonists pay for the costs of the war.

- In 1764, a Sugar Act was brought in to tax sugar.
- A year later, the Stamp Act placed a tax on printed materials.
- The Quartering Act required Americans to house and feed British troops.

Americans throughout the thirteen colonies protested against 'taxation without representation'. They were expected to pay taxes, and yet had no vote in the British Parliament.

Boston Tea Party

In 1773, the British Parliament passed a Tea Act. They allowed one tea company the sole right to sell tea to the colonies. The Americans were furious and refused to unload the ships. On the night of 16 December 1773, sixty men disguised as Native Americans boarded the ships. They dumped the entire shipment of tea overboard into Boston Harbour. This event is famously known as the Boston Tea Party.

The British king, George III, wanted to punish the Americans after the Boston Tea Party. A new set of laws was passed. Boston Harbour was closed and no food could be shipped in.

Word Watch!
Colonists were people who settled in a new country but remained loyal to their parent state.

Fast Facts!
King George III was the ruler of England from 1760 to 1820. He is known as 'the king who lost America' because it was during this time that America became independent.

Children investigate revolution and change in America, France and Ireland, studying some of the different personalities, attitudes, events and developments in these periods.

41

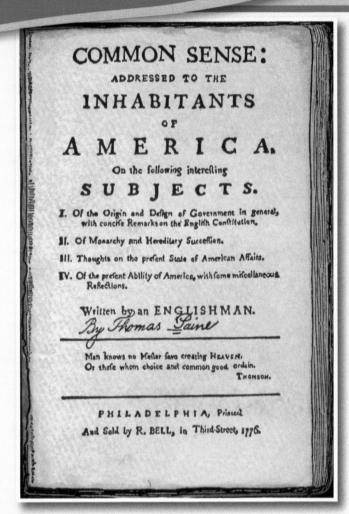

In January 1776, an Englishman, Thomas Paine, published a book called *Common Sense*. The book stated that all kings were unjust and encouraged America to be a free and independent nation.

The First Shot

On 19 April 1775, some British troops in Boston marched to the nearby town of Concord to seize guns and ammunition. They were attacked and the first shot was fired. The American War of Independence had begun. George Washington was voted as Commander-in-Chief of the new army.

War of Independence

On 4 July 1776, the American Congress issued the Declaration of Independence. They believed they had the right to 'life, liberty and the pursuit of happiness'. This showed Britain that America was determined to become a free nation. The Americans got money from France to help their side. France and Britain had been at war on and off for decades. France agreed to help the Americans as a way to attack Britain.

George Washington

On 9 October 1781, after six years, the Revolutionary War was over. The Americans and British signed a peace treaty in Paris in 1783. The United States of America was born. George Washington became the first president, in 1789.

The French Revolution

People in Europe had a great interest in the American Revolution. France had supported the Americans in the revolution. By 1787, the French government was bankrupt after several expensive wars. Many people accused the Queen, Marie Antoinette, of spending too much money on luxuries.

The wealthy people, the nobles and clergy, in France had many privileges and did not have to pay taxes. The peasants had to pay many taxes. They were hungry because of a lack of food from poor harvests. Finally, they took the law into their own hands.

The National Assembly

The middle and poorer classes grew tired of waiting for change. Up until now, the nobility and the clergy had controlled parliament. Now the people set up their own National Assembly. They represented 96 per cent of the people.

Storming of the Bastille

Rumours spread around Paris that the King was going to close down the National Assembly. On 14 July 1789, an angry mob rioted and attacked the prison called the Bastille. Prisoners were freed and weapons were taken.

The French Revolution had begun. In the countryside, peasants and farmers revolted by attacking the estates of their landlords. Today, 14 July is celebrated as a national holiday in France. It is called Bastille Day.

This cartoon was created in the 1780s. It helps to explain the causes of the French Revolution. Label the three figures in the cartoon: peasant, priest and noble. What is happening in the cartoon?

'Liberty, Equality and Fraternity' was the motto of the French Revolution.

Liberty · Equality · Fraternity

King Louis XVI and his wife, Queen Marie Antoinette, were sentenced to death and executed by guillotine.

Declaration of the Rights of Man
The National Assembly passed the Declaration of the Rights of Man on 4 August 1789. A new constitution was introduced in 1791. France was declared a Republic.

Declaration of the Rights of Man
- Men are born free and remain equal in rights.
- Man has rights to liberty, property, security and resistance to oppression.
- The free communication of ideas and opinions is one of the most precious of the rights of man.

Rebellion in Ireland

United Irishmen

Inspired by the American and French Revolution, the Society of the United Irishmen was set up in Belfast in October 1791. Theobald Wolfe Tone was its leader. He hoped to unite Catholics and Protestants and to reform the Irish Parliament. The organisation spread throughout Ireland and by 1797 there were 100,000 members. They now wanted an Irish Republic, like the French and Americans.

Help from France

The leaders of the United Irishmen hoped to postpone a rebellion until French weapons and troops could land and help their cause. In December 1796, Wolfe Tone brought 15,000 French troops to Bantry Bay. Unfortunately, bad storms prevented them landing and they returned to France. The British Government introduced Martial Law from 2 March 1797. As the soldiers search for weapons, they burned houses. Many acts of violence such as pitchcapping, torture and murder were carried out in a wave of terror.

Theobald Wolfe Tone

Fast Facts!

Other leaders of the United Irishmen were Thomas Russell, Henry Joy McCracken and William Drennan.

Word Watch!
Martial law

The army, or military, takes over the rule of law in the absence of civil law.

This drawing shows Captain Swayne from the Cork Militia carrying out an act of pitchcapping. Hot pitch or tar is poured onto the victim's head.

The Date is Set

With several United Irishmen leaders arrested, it was decided to proceed with the rebellion without French aid. The date was set for 23 May 1798. Informers leaked the plans to the British but the counties surrounding Dublin rose as planned. The Rising had finally begun on the morning of 24 May.

1798 Rebellion

The Government successfully put down most of the rebel attacks. Rebels were defeated in Kildare, Carlow and Meath. Rebels in the North East were led by McCracken. At first they won some battles but their success was short lived.

Many rebels came out to fight in Wicklow and they had the most success in Wexford. Fr John Murphy from Boolavogue led the local rebels. They captured Enniscorthy, but failed to take New Ross. The Battle of Vinegar Hill took place on 21 June. The rebels were defeated in a bloody battle.

> **Boolavogue**
>
> At Boolavogue, as the sun was setting
> O'er the bright May meadows of Shelmalier
> A rebel hand set the heather blazing
> And brought the neighbours from far and near.
>
> Then Father Murphy, from old Kilcormack,
> Spurred up the rocks with a warning cry.
> 'Arm, Arm,' he cried, 'for I've come to lead you
> For Ireland's freedom we fight or die.'

Many popular songs and ballads were written about the 1798 Rebellion.

French help too late

Nearly two months after the Rebellion, 1,000 French soldiers landed in Co. Mayo. It had been too late. The Act of Union in 1800 ended the Irish parliament and brought Ireland tighter under British control. Almost 30,000 people had been killed in the Rebellion.

The Battle of Vinegar Hill

Question Time

1 Why did British Parliament introduce taxes?
2 List some of the taxes introduced.
3 Why, do you think, are there 13 stripes on the American flag?
4 Why do Americans celebrate Independence Day on 4 July each year?
5 When did the Boston Tea Party occur?
6 Describe the Boston Tea Party.
7 Who was the leader of the colonial army?
8 Who wrote the book *Common Sense*?
9 Why was the French government bankrupt?
10 Why is 14 July a national holiday in France today?
11 What was the motto of the French Revolution?
12 Who were the United Irishmen?
13 When did the Rebellion take place in Ireland?

Creative Time

1 Imagine that you are a colonist living in America. Write a letter to the British Parliament to convince them to change the unfair taxes.

2 People in the colonies learned about the Boston Tea Party from posters. Design your own poster retelling the events of the Boston Tea Party.

3 Write your own revolution ballad encouraging the people to keep fighting for freedom.

4 You are a journalist working in Paris in 1789. Write the front page of the newspaper article describing the storming of the Bastille.

Puzzle Time

Match the following words to their correct meaning.

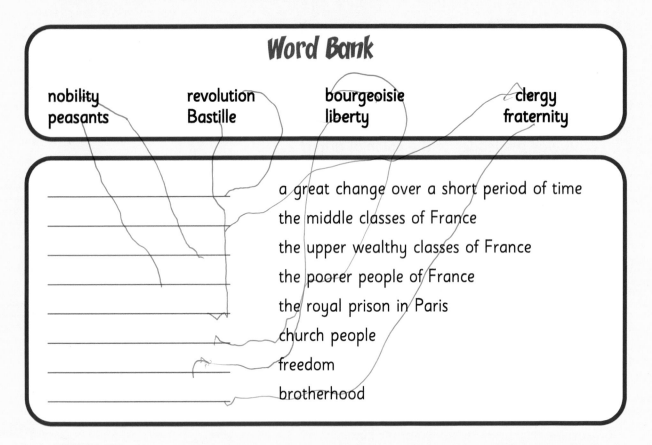

Word Bank

nobility   revolution   bourgeoisie   clergy
peasants   Bastille   liberty   fraternity

_____ a great change over a short period of time

_____ the middle classes of France

_____ the upper wealthy classes of France

_____ the poorer people of France

_____ the royal prison in Paris

_____ church people

_____ freedom

_____ brotherhood

Time Detective

1 Visit the National Library or use the Internet to investigate the Rebellion of 1798. Look at this website: http://www.nationalarchives.ie/PDF/1798.pdf . Working as an historian, you can download many of the original documents available from that time.

2 The Rebellion of 1798 gave rise to many poems and ballads. Visit a music shop or use the Internet to find some more of these. Here is one website that may be useful: http://www.iol.ie/~98com/ballads.htm

English

Choose one revolutionary that you would like to interview.

Write your questions and act out the interview in pairs.

Gaeilge

Léigh an dán 'Bás an Chroipí' bunaithe ar 1798 ar

http://www.iol.ie/~98com/ballads.htm

Mathematics

In Ireland, we pay tax on our earnings.

What is the current rate of tax?

What tax do you pay on items bought?

Drama

Recreate the Boston Tea Party. Write a short play retelling the story of this event.

Take on the role of the key people involved in the Boston Tea Party and present your play to your class.

Revolution and Change

Geography

On a map of the world, plot the location of the different revolutions described in this chapter.

Music

The 1798 Rebellion inspired many ballads and songs.

Listen to songs such as 'Boolavogue' and 'Kelly the boy from Killanne'.

Art

Design your own postage stamp to celebrate the anniversary of a revolution of your choice.

Science

Have a tea tasting afternoon. Try many different types of tea such as herbal, earl grey, lemon tea, green tea, etc.

Can you identify and name the different teas?

In 1845, over eight million people lived in Ireland. More than half the population lived in small mud cabins on tiny plots of land. They were an agricultural society and depended on the potato crop. Landlords owned the land and many lived in Britain. They were known as absentee landlords. Since the Act of Union in 1800, Ireland no longer had its own parliament and was ruled from London. Often, decisions were made about Ireland by people who did not understand the Irish situation. The Great Famine, An Gorta Mór, of 1845–51, was one of the worst tragedies in Irish history.

The Potato

The potato was first brought to Ireland by Sir Walter Raleigh. The climate here suited potato-growing. Potatoes were popular because they needed little space, equipment or skill to grow. This nutritious food yielded a high crop and was cheap. Potatoes were eaten for breakfast, dinner and supper. An average man ate 6½ kg a day of potatoes (70 potatoes). Failure of the potato crop would mean disaster as over 3 million people lived on a diet of potatoes only.

Potato Quiz!

1 How many different types of potatoes can you name?
2 Before the famine, how many potatoes were eaten on a daily basis?
3 How many potatoes were eaten every week? How many were eaten every year?
4 In your opinion, how many potatoes would a young person eat?
5 How, do you think, were the potatoes cooked?
6 Why, do you think, was it not good to rely on one main food source?

Disaster Strikes

In 1845, a disease called 'the blight' killed the potato crop. This fungus was spread by the wind. The potatoes turned black and soft. When these rotting potatoes were dug up, the smell was unbearable. The blight destroyed the main food source for many people. As a result, one in eight people died. The British government had a policy of *laissez faire*, which meant 'leave be'. Many months passed before it admitted help was needed. The government left the responsibility of feeding the poor to different charities.

Study this picture of the cabin of J. Donoghue and answer the following questions:

1 What is the cabin made from?
2 What animals do the Donoghue family have?
3 How is food cooked?
4 Why, do you think, is there a hole in the roof?
5 Write a thought bubble for each of the members of the Donoghue family showing what they are thinking.

Under the Hawthorn Tree by Marita Conlon-McKenna

Read the following passage from this book, which is set in Ireland during the Great Famine.

Eily could feel tears at the back of her eyes. Sometimes she thought that maybe this was all a dream and soon she would wake up and laugh at it, but the hunger pain in her tummy and the sadness in her heart were enough to know that it was real. She closed her eyes and remembered.

It was hard to believe that it was only a little over a year ago, and they sitting in the old school room, when Tim O'Kelly had run in to get his brother John and told them all to 'Make a run home quick to help with lifting the spuds as a pestilence had fallen on the place and they were rotting in the ground.'

They all waited for the master to get his stick and shout at Tim: Away out of it, you fool, to disturb the learning, but were surprised when he shut his book and told them to make haste and 'Mind, no dawdling,' and 'Away home to give a hand.' They all ran so fast that their breath caught in their throats, half afraid of what they would find at home.

Eily remembered. Father was sitting on the stone wall, his head in his hands. Mother was kneeling in the field, her hands and apron covered in mud as she pulled the potatoes from the ground, and all around the air heavy with a smell — a smell, rotting horrible, up your nose, in your mouth. The smell of badness and disease.

Across the valley the men cursed and the woman prayed to God to save them. Field after field of potatoes had died and rotted in the ground. The crop, their food-crop was gone. All the children stared — eyes large and frightened, for even they knew that now the hunger would come.

Imagine that you are Eily living in the time of the Great Famine.
- Write a diary entry.
- What are your worries and concerns?
- What are you thinking?

1846 – Crop Fails Again

Despite the hopes for a successful crop, the potato crop failed again in 1846. Starving people ate whatever food they could find. Some even had to eat grass to survive.

Relief

In 1845–46, the British Prime Minister, Sir Robert Peel, organised some aid. He set up a commission to investigate the problem. Indian corn was bought from America to feed the poor. This was to be sold cheaply. However, many people did not even have the money to buy the corn. Relief schemes such as canal and road building were set up to provide work for the people. Workers were paid at the end of the week. Some died of starvation before ever receiving their wages.

Throughout the famine, while people were dying of starvation, food was being exported. This food could have kept people alive. In Dungarvan, Co. Waterford, police fired on a crowd that were trying to stop grain leaving the port. Several people were injured and one man died.

Study this picture carefully and answer the following questions:

1 What is being loaded onto the ship?
2 Where is the ship headed for?
3 Why are the British army guarding the ship?
4 Why are the people on the docks so angry?
5 Choose two people from the picture. Write the conversation you think they might be having.

Black '47

1847 was the worst year of the famine. Diseases such as typhus, cholera, dysentery and scurvy spread. More people died from sickness and disease than from starvation. Families were found dead in cabins. Their bodies were eaten by starving cats and dogs. There were widespread evictions as people could not afford to pay their rent.

The Workhouses

Workhouses were built all over Ireland in the 1830s and 1840s. They were built to help people who could not help themselves. There were over 130 workhouses set up all over Ireland. People hated going to the workhouses but they were left with no other choice because conditions were so bad. As a result, the workhouses were overcrowded with people waiting at the gates to get in.

Conditions in the workhouses were terrible. Families were separated when they arrived. People were not allowed to leave the workhouse at any time. Men worked for ten hours a day breaking stones and the women had to knit. Little children got school lessons every day while older children had to work. There were strict rules in the workhouse – no bad language, no disobedience, no laziness, no talking during mealtimes – and families could not meet together except during mass on Sundays.

People trying to get into a workhouse

Choose one person from the picture and write some questions that you would like to ask him/her.

Soup Kitchens

Soup kitchens were set up to help to feed the poor. The Society of Friends, known as the Quakers, set up the first soup kitchen in Dublin. A litre of soup cost one penny. Those who could not afford to pay received their soup free. Later, the government set up soup kitchens all over Ireland. By August 1847, up to three million people were receiving soup daily. Soup kitchens saved many lives.

 Web Watch!

Read about the soup kitchens and some of the different recipes used to make the soup on this website: http://www.limerick.com/lifestyle/soupkitchen.html .

Create a freeze frame of this picture. Each person in your group takes on the role of a different person in the picture. Imagine that you are that person.

■ What are they thinking?

■ How are they feeling?

■ What are their thoughts and concerns?

You then freeze, recreating this picture. Each person in turn tells their thoughts.

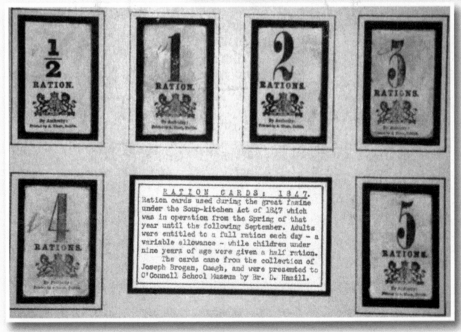

Soup Kitchen Ration Cards

The Effects

The population of Ireland was greatly reduced by the famine. More than one million people died and a further one and a half million emigrated. Thousands of people died on 'coffin ships'. This was the name given to the ships which carried people to other countries. The conditions on board these ships were terrible. The ships were overcrowded and many people did not have enough food or water to last for the whole voyage. Many children died and many more became orphans.

Fast Facts!

The famine also affected the use of the Irish language. Many of the poorer families who died or emigrated spoke Irish so there was a huge decline in the use of the Irish language.

Famine Today

Many years on, there are still famines in the world. While there is plenty of food on the planet for everyone, some countries still have food shortages. We often hear of famines in other countries on the news. These are often caused by water shortages, disease in crops, or war. Many organisations help those affected by famine. We are often asked to give generously to these organisations.

Famine victims in Somalia wait in line for food.

Question Time

1   When did the Great Famine take place?
2   What was the Act of Union?
3   What was an absentee landlord?
4   Why were potatoes a popular crop to grow in Ireland?
5   What happened to the potato crops? Why was this such a disaster for ordinary people?
6   What were soup kitchens?
7   What were coffin ships? Why, do you think, did they get this name?
8   Name some of the diseases that killed people during the famine.
9   What were the effects of the famine?

Creative Time

Drama time!

Imagine that it is the time of the Great Famine. People are starving. A local meeting has been called in the town hall to discuss the problem. Divide your class into small groups. Each group takes on the role of a different group of people living in Ireland at that time. They must speak at the meeting, giving their suggestions to help solve the problem. It is important to get your point across about your worries and fears if something is not done.

Here are some possible groups:
- Improving Landlords (Good landlords who charged fair rent and put money back into the land)
- Absentee Landlords
- Tenant farmers
- Labourers
- Children of labourers
- Head of a Workhouse
- Head of a Soup Kitchen

Puzzle Time

Cause or Effect

Some of these sentences are **causes** of the famine, why it happened.
Others are **effects**, things that happened as a result of the famine.
Write 'cause' or 'effect' after each sentence.

1 The people depended mainly on one crop, the potato. _cause_

2 Over one million people died as a result of the Great Famine. _effect_

3 Over one million people emigrated as a result of the famine. _effect_

4 Ireland was ruled by a government in London. _cause_

5 Many tenant farmers were evicted from their homes when
   they could not pay their rent. _effect_

6 The British government was slow to administer help. _cause_

7 There was a large population of poor people living in small
   mud cabins. They lived off a very small plot of land. _cause_

Time Detective

1 Working as an historian, investigate the effects of the famine
   in your locality. Find out where the nearest workhouse was in
   your area.

2 Research books in the library about the famine. Consider
   reading *Under the Hawthorn Tree* by Marita Conlon-
   McKenna, published by The O'Brien Press, or have a look at
   some of the documents from the Famine in the Education
   Packs by Dr Noel Kissane, *Irish Famine: A documentary
   history* (books and pamphlets available from the National
   Library of Ireland).

Web Watch!

See an interactive tour of the Irish Potato Famine on:

http://www.irishpotatofamine.org/flash.html

http://www.techlearning.com/webpicks/showArticle.php?articleID=192202601

Integration Project

English

Write your favourite potato recipe.

Create a class potato recipe book by putting all the recipes together.

Design a cover for your book.

Gaeilge

Leadóg Focal: Seasann beirt pháistí suas. Luann gach páiste cineál bia. Suíonn an páiste síos muna bhfuil focal aige/aici.

Mathematics

If 1 million people died and 1½ million people emigrated during the famine out of a population of 8 million:
- What percentage of the population died?
- What percentage emigrated?
- What percentage remained?
- Draw a pie chart showing these statistics.

Drama

Choose one image of the Great Famine such as workhouses, soup kitchens or emigration.
Working in small groups, create a still image of this scene. Your classmates can try to guess which scene you are recreating.

An Gorta Mór

Geography

Investigate natural disasters of the modern world such as the Tsunami in Thailand or Hurricane Katrina in New Orleans.

Which natural disaster cost the most lives?

Which cost the most in damages?

Which lasted the longest?

Music

'The Fields of Athenry' is a song about famine times.

Listen to the words and learn the song.

Art

Select one image that stands out for you from the Great Famine.

Using charcoal, draw this famine scene.

Science

Starch is white and odourless. If starch is present in food, the food will turn purple when an iodine solution is put on it. Test the following foods for starch: rice, potato, apple, orange and bread.

In the late 19th century and early 1900s, people began to take a greater interest and a greater pride in their own country. This is called nationalism. Some Irish people were not happy with the increasing English influence in Ireland. Traditional Irish pastimes and customs had been in decline. The Irish language was no longer the most widely spoken language. Famine and emigration meant that many Irish speaking people had died or left the country.

Word Watch!
Irish Cultural Revival
New organisations were founded to encourage a passion for Irish customs and traditions. People began to take a new pride and interest in their country.

The Gaelic Athletic Association (G A A)

In November 1884, Michael Cusack founded the Gaelic Athletic Association. The GAA encouraged the playing of Irish games and drew up rules showing how these games should be played. Maurice Davin was the first president of the GAA.

The GAA spread quickly through the countryside. Hurling, Gaelic football, handball and rounders were encouraged. Members were banned from playing non-Gaelic games such as rugby or cricket. Members of the Royal Irish Constabulary (RIC) and the British Army were banned from becoming members. The first All-Ireland Championships in hurling and Gaelic football were organised in 1887. Twelve of the thirty-two counties entered — five competed in hurling and eight in football. A national stadium was built and named Croke Park after its patron, Archbishop Croke of Cashel.

Michael Cusack

Children investigate the GAA, the Gaelic League and the literary revival, exploring the impact they had on the lives of Irish people during the late 19th and early 20th centuries.

1887: Tipperary team in first All-Ireland Hurling Final

1897: Dublin team in Dr Croke Cup Football Final

Study the two photographs above.

1 How do the uniforms worn in the past compare with those worn today?
2 What differences are there in terms of safety?
3 Which uniforms do you prefer? Why?
4 What footwear are the men wearing?

The Gaelic League (Conradh na Gaeilge)

Along with a decline in Irish games and customs, there was also a decline in the use of the Irish language. After the famine, there was a major reduction in people speaking Irish. Many native Irish speakers left Ireland to seek work in other countries. In 1890, only 14 per cent of Irish people could speak Irish. Parents discouraged their children from speaking the language. Many thought English would be the language of the future.

Douglas Hyde

> **Preliminary meeting**
>
> At a meeting held on Monday, 13 July 1893, at 9 Lower O'Connell street, Dublin. Douglas Hyde LL.D. in the chair, the following also present:
>
> Chas Percy Bushe John McNeill BA
> Jas Michl Cogan Patrick O'Brien.
> Thos W Ellerker T. O'Neill Russell.
> Rev. Wm Hayden S.J. Fitzgerald?
> Patrick J Hogan, M.A.
> Martin Kelly
>
> It was moved by JMcNeill seconded by JM Cogan and resolved
>
> That a Society be formed under the name of the Gaelic League for the purpose of keeping the Irish Language spoken in Ireland.
>
> Moved by J O'Neill Russell, seconded by M Kelly and resolved unanimously.
>
> That we here present constitute ourselves into a Society under the name and for the purpose aforesaid

Study the document opposite and answer the following questions.

1 When was the meeting held?
2 Where was the meeting held?
3 Who attended the meeting?
4 Who was the chairperson of the meeting?

In 1893, Douglas Hyde and Eoin Mac Neill founded the Gaelic League. Its aim was to preserve and restore Irish as a spoken language. By 1905, it had 550 branches throughout the country. The branches organised Irish classes, concerts and dances.

From 1899, the Gaelic League published an Irish-language newspaper called *An Claidheamh Soluis (The Sword of Light)*. The Gaelic League made people more aware of their culture. It was also successful in having Irish taught in National Schools.

Pádraig Pearse

Pádraig Pearse joined the Gaelic League and he was the editor of An Claidheamh Soluis from 1903 to 1909. He was a teacher who was interested in promoting the Irish language. He founded Coláiste Éanna and Coláiste Íde in Dublin, schools which were devoted to the education of children through the Irish language. Later, he was to become one of the leaders of the 1916 Easter Rising.

Irish Literature

At this time, there was also a growth in Irish literature. Although this was often written in English, it was based on Irish themes. The poet W.B. Yeats wrote poems and dramas that were inspired by Irish myths and legends. The Irish National Theatre, the Abbey, was formed by Yeats and Lady Gregory to put on Irish plays. It opened its doors on 27 December 1904 for the first time. Yeats was awarded the Nobel Prize for Literature in 1923.

W.B. Yeats

Lady Gregory

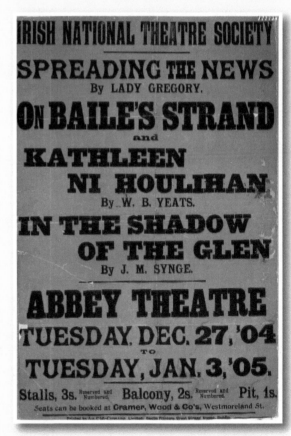

IRISH NATIONAL THEATRE SOCIETY

SPREADING THE NEWS
By LADY GREGORY.

ON BAILE'S STRAND
and

KATHLEEN NI HOULIHAN
By W. B. YEATS.

IN THE SHADOW OF THE GLEN
By J. M. SYNGE.

ABBEY THEATRE
TUESDAY. DEC. 27, '04
TO
TUESDAY, JAN. 3, '05.

Stalls, 3s. Reserved and Numbered. Balcony, 2s. Reserved and Numbered. Pit, 1s.
Seats can be booked at Cramer, Wood & Co's, Westmoreland St.

Study the poster for the opening of the Abbey Theatre opposite.

1 When did the Abbey theatre first open?
2 What plays were showing?
3 What dates were the plays running?
4 How much did a seat in the balcony cost?

Irish Art

The Arts and Craft Society of Ireland was founded in 1894.
This encouraged Irish artists to present their work in exhibitions.

Question Time

1. Why, do you think, was there a decline in Irish customs and pastimes?
2. Who founded the Gaelic Athletic Association?
3. What were the aims of the Association?
4. What games were banned by the GAA?
5. Why was the National Stadium named Croke Park?
6. Why, do you think, was there a decline in the Irish language?
7. Why was the Gaelic League founded?
8. What were the aims of the Gaelic League?
9. What was *An Claidheamh Soluis*? What does the name mean?
10. When was the Abbey Theatre opened?

Creative Time

1. Create a poster encouraging people to join the Gaelic League. What were its aims? How would you convince people to join? What images would you draw? Remember to include a catchy title.

2. Imagine that you attended the first ever All-Ireland Hurling Final. Write a report about the game, the atmosphere and how you felt attending this historic match.

3. Here is the poem 'He Wishes for the Cloths of Heaven' and the first verse of 'The Lake Isle of Innisfree'. Read a selection of poems by W.B. Yeats and choose your favourite. Give reasons for your choice.

He Wishes for the Cloths of Heaven

Had I the heavens' embroidered cloths,
Enwrought with golden and silver light,
The blue and the dim and the dark cloths
Of night and light and the half-light,
I would spread the cloths under your feet:
But I, being poor, have only my dreams;
I have spread my dreams under your feet;
Tread softly because you tread upon my dreams.

The Lake Isle of Innisfree

I will arise and go now, and go to Innisfree,
And a small cabin build there, of clay and wattles made:
Nine bean-rows will I have there, a hive for the honey-bee,
And live alone in the bee-loud glade.

Puzzle Time

Using the Internet or programmes from GAA matches, research the history of the All-Ireland Finals in hurling and football.

Match the county to the year it won the All-Ireland Football Final:

2007	Galway
2004	Dublin
2003	Kerry
2001	Meath
1996	Donegal
1995	Kerry
1992	Tyrone

Time Detective

1 Working as an historian, investigate the history of your local GAA club.
   ■ When was it founded?
   ■ How did it get its name?
   ■ Were there any historic events that happened there?
   Gather any old photographs or documents about the club.
   Create a poster to present your information in the classroom.

2 The GAA and Conradh na Gaeilge are two organisations that promote the Irish language and traditions. Select one of these organisations. Find out as much information as you can about it and present your findings as a class project.

Web Watch!

www.gaa.ie
http://www.cnag.ie/

Integration Project

Irish Cultural Revival

English

Choose two teams to debate this topic: 'Irish should be a compulsory subject up to Leaving Certificate'.

Gaeilge

Déan póstaer chun daoine a spreagadh le bheith ag caint Gaeilge. Cur suas na póstaeir ar phasáistí na scoile.

Mathematics

Create a bar chart highlighting the amount of times that different counties have won the All-Ireland Football and Hurling Championships. You could include some questions with your graph. Visit:

http://www.cul4kidz.com/culstats_aititles.htm

Drama

Hot Seat: One member of the class takes on the role of Douglas Hyde and sits in the 'Hot Seat'.

Take it in turns to ask him questions about his life.

Geography

How well do you know the colours of Ireland's counties?

Try the quiz on:
http://82.141.251.115/res/Crosswords/amm56pegaafoot.html

Music

Write a rap song about your county. Include a chorus and two verses.

You could use some musical instruments to accompany your rap.

Art

Design a new jersey for your county.

What colours would you choose?

What images would you include on your jersey?

Science

Investigate friction. Carry out a fair test using a football/*sliotar* to see how they travel on different surfaces. Roll the ball with the same force on different surfaces such as glass, carpet, wood, grass and cement. Make predictions. Then measure how far they travel.

The Easter Rising of 1916 was a major event in Irish history. It made people think more urgently about the question of Irish independence. Since the Act of Union in 1800, Ireland had been under British rule. When World War I began in 1914, some Irish people thought that this was the time to make plans for an uprising against the British. They saw England's difficulty as Ireland's opportunity. In May 1915, a Military Council was formed and set about organising arms for a rebellion. The rebels who took part in the Rising were from different organisations.

Irish Republican Brotherhood (IRB)

The Irish Republican Brotherhood was established in 1858. Its goal was the creation of an Irish Republic with the use of arms if necessary. The IRB was a secret society and had a key role in planning the 1916 Rising.

Irish Volunteers

The Irish Volunteers were founded in 1913. Members of the IRB also joined the Irish Volunteers. Eoin Mac Neill was the leader of the Volunteers.

Irish Citizen Army

The Irish Citizen Army was formed in 1913 by James Connolly. It was set up after a workers' strike to protect the workers and strikers. The Citizen Army was prepared to fight for independence to improve the lives of working people.

Cumann na mBan

Women played an important role in the 1916 Rising. Cumann na mBan, the women's organisation, was set up in 1914. During the Rising, women looked after first aid, prepared and delivered meals, and carried arms and information across the city. Countess Markievicz fought with the rebels at the College of Surgeons and St Stephen's Green.

Children investigate the 1916 Rising, examining the major personalities, events and developments in this key period in Irish history.

67

Disaster Strikes

The Military Council of the IRB secretly organised and planned the Rising. The members of the Military Council were Pádraig Pearse, Eamonn Ceannt, Joseph Plunkett, Thomas Clarke, Seán Mac Dermott, James Connolly and Thomas Mac Donagh. Easter Sunday 1916 was the date set for the Rising. This date was very significant as it tied in with the Easter religious celebration to mark the rising of Christ from the dead.

Sir Roger Casement went to Germany to organise arms for the rebellion. The German ship *The Aud* arrived off the coast of Kerry on Holy Thursday. The ship was intercepted by the British and the captain sunk the ship. All the arms sank to the bottom of the sea. When Eoin Mac Neill heard of the failed arms landing and the plans for the Rising, he issued orders cancelling all activities for Easter Sunday. There was confusion over these orders and the Rising had to be delayed. The new date set for the Rising was Easter Monday, 1916.

Sunday Independent, 23 April

Owing to the very critical position, all orders given to Irish Volunteers for tomorrow, Easter Sunday, are hereby rescinded and no parades, marches, or other movement of Irish Volunteers will take place. Each individual Volunteer will obey this order strictly in every particular.

Eoin Mac Neill

Eoin Mac Neill's orders cancelling activities for Easter Sunday

Eoin Mac Neill

James Connolly

Countess Markievicz

Monday 24 April

On a bright, sunny bank holiday Easter Monday, hundreds of volunteers gathered at Liberty Hall before marching to various buildings around Dublin. As well as rifles, some of the rebels carried pikes, sledge hammers and axes. They seized many key buildings around the city centre such as the GPO, The Four Courts, Boland's Mill, St Stephen's Green, Jacob's Factory and the South Dublin Union. The rebels were unsuccessful in gaining control of Dublin Castle.

People walking along Sackville Street, now O'Connell Street, did not know what was happening. Two flags were raised above the GPO – a tricolour and a green flag with the words 'Irish Republic' on it. Pádraig Pearse declared the establishment of an Irish Republic on the steps of the GPO. He read the Proclamation of Independence to a puzzled crowd.

Irish Republic Flag

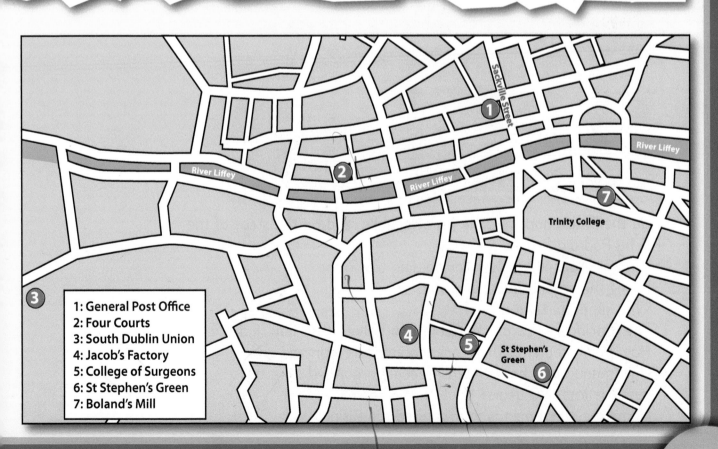

1: General Post Office
2: Four Courts
3: South Dublin Union
4: Jacob's Factory
5: College of Surgeons
6: St Stephen's Green
7: Boland's Mill

POBLACHT NA H EIREANN.
THE PROVISIONAL GOVERNMENT
OF THE
IRISH REPUBLIC.
TO THE PEOPLE OF IRELAND.

IRISHMEN AND IRISHWOMEN: In the name of God and of the dead generations from which she receives her old tradition of nationhood, Ireland, through us, summons her children to her flag and strikes for her freedom.

Having organised and trained her manhood through her secret revolutionary organisation, the Irish Republican Brotherhood, and through her open military organisations, the Irish Volunteers and the Irish Citizen Army, having patiently perfected her discipline, having resolutely waited for the right moment to reveal itself, she now seizes that moment, and, supported by her exiled children in America and by gallant allies in Europe, but relying in the first on her own strength, she strikes in full confidence of victory.

We declare the right of the people of Ireland to the ownership of Ireland, and to the unfettered control of Irish destinies, to be sovereign and indefeasible. The long usurpation of that right by a foreign people and government has not extinguished the right, nor can it ever be extinguished except by the destruction of the Irish people. In every generation the Irish people have asserted their right to national freedom and sovereignty; six times during the past three hundred years they have asserted it in arms. Standing on that fundamental right and again asserting it in arms in the face of the world, we hereby proclaim the Irish Republic as a Sovereign Independent State, and we pledge our lives and the lives of our comrades-in-arms to the cause of its freedom, of its welfare, and of its exaltation among the nations.

The Irish Republic is entitled to, and hereby claims, the allegiance of every Irishman and Irishwoman. The Republic guarantees religious and civil liberty, equal rights and equal opportunities to all its citizens, and declares its resolve to pursue the happiness and prosperity of the whole nation and of all its parts, cherishing all the children of the nation equally, and oblivious of the differences carefully fostered by an alien government, which have divided a minority from the majority in the past.

Until our arms have brought the opportune moment for the establishment of a permanent National Government, representative of the whole people of Ireland and elected by the suffrages of all her men and women, the Provisional Government, hereby constituted, will administer the civil and military affairs of the Republic in trust for the people.

We place the cause of the Irish Republic under the protection of the Most High God, Whose blessing we invoke upon our arms, and we pray that no one who serves that cause will dishonour it by cowardice, inhumanity, or rapine. In this supreme hour the Irish nation must, by its valour and discipline and by the readiness of its children to sacrifice themselves for the common good, prove itself worthy of the august destiny to which it is called.

Signed on Behalf of the Provisional Government,

THOMAS J. CLARKE.

SEAN Mac DIARMADA. THOMAS MacDONAGH.
P. H. PEARSE, EAMONN CEANNT,
JAMES CONNOLLY. JOSEPH PLUNKETT.

Study the Proclamation of the Irish Republic read on the steps of the GPO by Pádraig Pearse.

1 What reasons were given for holding the Rising?
2 Name the organisations involved.
3 Who supported the rebels?
4 The Proclamation was printed in two halves. Can you find the divide?
5 How many copies of the Proclamation were printed?
6 How many times have the Irish people organised uprisings over the last 300 years?
7 Name the **seven** men who organised the Rising.

Tuesday 25 April

British army reinforcements came from Belfast, Templemore and Athlone. The rebels were outnumbered. The army placed a cordon round the city to isolate the rebels from each other. The British attacked St Stephen's Green, forcing the rebels to flee. Looting became widespread as people robbed from city shops.

GPO after the shelling

Wednesday 26 April

Army reinforcements from England arrived but met rebels at Mount Street Bridge. The British gunboat *Helga* sailed up the Liffey and began shelling Liberty Hall and the GPO. There was major damage to buildings. Fierce fighting continued across Dublin.

Thursday 27 April

The military were now in control with the cordon around the GPO continuing to tighten. Sackville Street was still under attack with much of the street in flames. James Connolly was shot in the ankle but continued to direct military operations.

Damaged buildings in Dublin, 1916

Friday 28 April

The GPO was in flames, with parts of the roof collapsing. The rebels had to evacuate the building. Pearse and Connolly were the last to leave, with Connolly being carried on a stretcher because of his injuries. By Friday night, the GPO was nothing more than a shell.

Saturday 29 April

Pádraig Pearse agreed to surrender to prevent further loss of life. Nurse Elizabeth O'Farrell waved a white flag for surrender. All rebels were instructed to lay down their weapons and line up in Sackville Street.

Pádraig Pearse surrenders

The Easter Rising brought much death and destruction. It is reported that 142 British soldiers and police and 64 rebels were killed, while 254 civilians were killed during the week. Over 2,000 people were injured in the fighting. Most of the fighting took place in Dublin. However, other areas also were involved. In Ashbourne, Co. Meath, Enniscorthy, Co. Wexford and Galway city there was significant fighting.

After the Rising, the people of Dublin were angry with the rebels for the destruction caused. Many jeered as the rebels were marched through the streets to prison. The British army decided to deal with the rebels in a tough manner. Over 3,000 people were arrested. Ninety people were sentenced to death. Fifteen of them, including the seven signatories of the Proclamation, were executed by firing squad. An injured James Connolly was strapped to a chair before being shot.

The executions changed public opinion. Soon, the rebels were seen as heroes. The Government had to react to this change of mood. Seventy-five of the death sentences were changed to sentences of life imprisonment.

Sackville Street before and after the 1916 Rising

Study the two photographs of Sackville Street in 1916.

1 What buildings or statues do you recognise?

2 What buildings remained untouched after the 1916 Rising?

3 What damage was done by the Rising?

4 What methods of transport were used in 1916?

5 Imagine that two ordinary people in Sackville Street are going to the GPO. Write the conversation they might be having about the Rising.

Question Time

1 In what year did World War I begin? *1915*
2 Name the different organisations that took part in the Rising. *IBRA ANO*
3 Who set up the Irish Citizen Army? Why? *te Frbe... nprSh Goionner*
4 Why was the date for the Rising changed? *Sbrll... Stan nprcomgb*
5 Was the British army ready for a Rising on Easter Monday? *ther Found or*
6 Where was the headquarters of the rebels in 1916? *Dvbln*
7 Name some of the buildings taken over by the rebels. *Gpo four courts*
8 What was O'Connell Street called in 1916? *SackVille St*
9 Why, do you think, was the civilian loss of life so high? *G ome anoment*
10 How long did the Rising last? *3 bays*
11 What was the public's opinion about the Rising? What changed this?
GaD Bue onen they Kive b people

Creative Time

1 You are a news reporter working for a national radio station.
Prepare a live news broadcast to be delivered from Sackville Street
during the Easter Rising. What important news updates will you feature?
2 Imagine that you are a rebel based in the GPO. Write your
daily diary entries for the week of the Rising.
   ■ What were your experiences?
   ■ Were you afraid?
   ■ What did you see?
   ■ Who did you meet?

Puzzle Time

True or False?

1 James Connolly set up the IRB. ✓ _____
2 The Military Council of the IRB planned the Rising. ✓ _____
3 World War I began in 1916. ✓ _____
4 The Rebels' headquarters were in Dublin Castle. ✗ _____
5 Pádraig Pearse read the Proclamation on the steps of the GPO. ✓ _____
6 Roger Casement went to Germany to organise arms for a Rising. ✓ _____
7 The Easter Rising brought much death and destruction. ✓ _____

Time Detective

Working as an historian, study these Irish newspapers reporting on the 1916 Rising.

The Belfast Newsletter, Tuesday 2 May 1916

The latest news about the Sinn Féin rising is good. On Sunday, General Maxwell informed a group of Press representatives that the back of the rising was broken, but not yet over...

Irish Independent, Thursday, 4 May 1916

No terms of denunciation that pen could indict would be too strong to apply to those responsible for the insane and criminal rising of last week...

The Irish Times, Thursday, 4 May 1916

The Rising was 'a criminal adventure. The leaders deserve little sympathy...'

The Freeman's Journal

Such a reckless and barren waste of life, courage, property and the historic beauty of a capital city.

1 What was the opinion of the newspapers about the Rising?
2 Were these newspapers neutral in their coverage of the 1916 Rising?
3 What would later cause them to change their opinion?
4 Choose one newspaper article and write the rest of the report.

Web Watch!

An interactive exhibition of the 1916 Rising is available from the National Library of Ireland on this website:
http://www.nli.ie/1916/1916_main.html

Hear personal accounts of 1916 at:
http://www.bbc.co.uk/history/british/easterrising/radio/index_js.shtml

Integration Project

English

Read some poems about 1916 such as *The Mother* by Pádraig Pearse.
Pearse wrote this poem the night before his execution in 1916.
His brother was also executed several days later.

Gaeilge

Déan dráma beag bunaithe ar léamh Fhorógra na Saoirse ar staighre an GPO.
Lig ort go raibh tú ann agus déan comhrá i mbeirteanna faoinar tharla ansin.

Mathematics

Create your own secret code that could have been used to inform the rebels about the Rising.

Start with a number that represents 'A', the next number represents 'B', etc. For example, A=5; B=6; C=7; D=8...

See if your friends can crack the code.

Drama

Conscience Alley:
The class forms two lines facing each other. One child walks down the line taking on the role of Eoin Mac Neill. Each child gives him advice as to whether or not to cancel the Rising.

Easter Rising 1916

Geography

Draw your own map of Dublin, marking in the seven rebel stations. Include modern landmarks to help you locate these buildings.

Music

Listen to the song *Grace*.

It is based on the marriage of Grace Gifford to Joseph Plunkett in the chapel at Kilmainham Gaol before the execution of Plunkett in 1916.

Art

Design your own cover for the book by Gerard Whelan *The Guns of Easter* published by The O'Brien Press.

What image will you draw?

What information should be included on the cover?

Science

It is the year 2016.
Design a building to commemorate the 100th anniversary of the 1916 Rising.

Draw the plans for this building.

People have celebrated feasts and festivals for centuries. Different festivals are celebrated all over the world.

It is believed that the first festivals came about because ancient societies wished to keep the forces of nature happy. Most ancient celebrations were linked with planting and harvest times or with honouring the dead. There are many religious celebrations. Some festivals mark an historic event such as a country gaining independence, or they can honour important people who are national heroes.

Traditions and stories can be passed on from one generation to another through the celebration of festivals. They help to keep memories alive.

Brainstorm
List some of the feasts and festivals that you celebrate.
How do you celebrate these feasts and festivals?
What other feast and festivals do you know about?
Discuss feasts or festivals with your class.
Write some questions about other festivals.

St Patrick's Day Parade, Christchurch, Dublin

Children explore feasts and festivals celebrated in Ireland and throughout the world.

Thanksgiving (USA)
Thanksgiving is celebrated on the fourth Thursday in November. It marks the arrival of the first English settlers to America.

Hallowe'en
Hallowe'en is celebrated in many countries. It may have come from the ancient Celtic festival called Samhain. The Celts celebrated the end of the harvest season by lighting bonfires to keep away evil spirits. Today, people dress up and play Hallowe'en games.

Independence Day (USA)
The fourth of July marks the signing of the Declaration of Independence in Philadelphia in 1776.

Day of the Dead (Mexico)
Mexicans celebrate 'Day of the Dead' on 1 November. Families gather together and pray for the souls of dead relatives. Mexicans decorate altars and visit cemeteries. Replicas of skeletons are also hung along the streets.

Carnival (Brazil)
Brazil's most popular festival is Carnival. This is celebrated on the Saturday before Ash Wednesday. People dress up in costumes and there are parades with music, fireworks and street performers.

Cocuk Bayrami (Turkey)
On 23 April, 'Children's Day' is celebrated in Turkey. Children dress up in special outfits or national costumes and parade through the streets.

St Lucia (Sweden)
The feast of St Lucia is celebrated on 13 December in Sweden. Children dress up and serve buns to their families.

Dyngus Day (Poland)
On Easter Monday in Poland, young people throw water at each other.

Chinese New Year
The Chinese New Year is the most important celebration in the Chinese calendar. It is usually celebrated for 14 days in January or February. People wear red clothes, give presents and set off firecrackers. A lantern festival marks the end of the celebrations. The dragon dance is the highlight of the festival.

Trung Thu (Vietnam)
This festival marks the end of harvest and the beauty of the full moon. Children wear colourful masks and dance in the streets with lit lanterns.

Esala Perahera (Sri Lanka)
This ten-day festival is held in August in honour of the Tooth Relic of Lord Buddha. There are parades with dancers, acrobats, flame throwers and elephants.

Diwali (India)
During the Hindu Festival of Lights, families come together and celebrate with gifts and feasts. Homes are decorated with lights from clay lamps.

Other Feasts and Festivals

Raksha Bandhan

This Hindu festival celebrates how important brothers and sisters are to each other. During a Rakhi ceremony, sisters put kum kum paste and rice on the foreheads of their brothers. Then they tie a special bracelet around their wrists called a rakhi. The brothers give gifts to their sisters and promise to protect and take care of them.

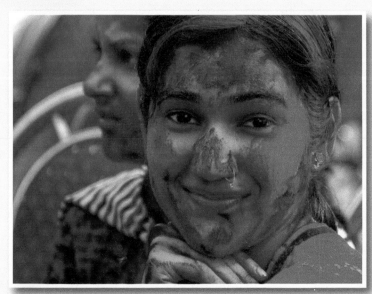

Ramadan

More than a billion Muslims all around the world take part in the fast of Ramadan. The fast lasts for a month. There is a meal before dawn and they do not eat again until darkness.

Holi

Holi is one of the most colourful festivals in the world. This Hindu festival is celebrated in early March. The night before Holi, fires are lit to keep away evil spirits. The next day people throw coloured powder at each other.

Yom Kippur

Yom Kippur is the most sacred of Jewish holidays. During this festival, Jewish people remember the past and apologise for any wrongdoings they may have done. This is also a time of fasting. The rabbi blows a shofar, a ram's horn, in the synagogue. This reminds the Jewish people of stories when the shofar was blown to announce an important event.

Hanukkah

Hanukkah is the Jewish festival of lights. It was first celebrated over 2,000 years ago in Judea, known today as Israel. It is celebrated in December and lasts for eight days. Candles are lit each day.

Hina Matsuri (Japan)

On 3 March, the Dolls' Festival is celebrated by girls in Japan. Families pray for the health and happiness of their daughters. Hina Dolls are displayed in homes.

Kodomono-hi (Japan)

A special day for boys in Japan is 5 May. They dress in kimonos and fly kites in the shape of fish.

Question Time

1 Why did the first festivals come about? *To worship and honour to entertener*
2 List some reasons why people celebrate feasts and festivals.
3 What Celtic festival did Hallowe'en come from? *Samhain*
4 When is Thanksgiving celebrated in the USA? *nov 4th*
5 Name a festival celebrated in Mexico. *Day of the dead*
6 Describe the celebrations that take place for the Chinese New Year. *Bright a nois*
7 Describe the Raksha Bandhan festival. *Lots of kids*
8 Name some festivals celebrated in Japan. *hina matsura*
9 Which festival would you most like to celebrate? *Hall*

Creative Time

1 Write a haiku about your favourite feast or festival. Take care counting the syllables.

2 Make a Chinese lantern to celebrate the Chinese New Year. All the lanterns can be hung from string across your classroom.

You will need:
- Coloured rectangular piece of paper
- Scissors
- Glue/tape or stapler

Method:
1 Fold the coloured piece of paper in half.
2 Make many cuts along the fold. Be careful not to cut all the way to the edge!
3 Unfold the paper and glue the top and bottom corners together.
4 To make a handle, cut a piece of paper 20cm long and 1cm wide. Glue to the top of the lantern.

Haiku

Here is a Japanese poem called a Haiku. It has three lines only. The first line has five syllables, the second has seven syllables and the last line has five syllables. It was written by Kijo Murakima (1865–1938).

First au-tumn morn-ing (5)
The mir-ror I stare in-to (7)
Shows my fa-ther's face (5)

Puzzle Time

Match the festival to its description.

Thanksgiving	One of the most colourful festivals
Independence Day	The Hindu festival of Lights
Day of the Dead	The arrival of first English settlers to the USA
Carnival	Young people throw water at each other
Raksha Bandhan	Children's Day in Turkey
Cocuk Bayrami	Hindu festival for brothers and sisters
Dyngus Day	Mexicans pray for the souls of dead relatives
Esala Perahera	Brazil's most popular festival
Trung Thu	American signing of Declaration of Independence
Hina Matsuri	The Jewish festival of lights
Diwali	The Japanese Dolls' Festival
Holi	Vietnamese festival to mark the end of harvest
Hanukkah	Festival to honour the Tooth Relic of Lord Buddha

Time Detective

Working as an historian, explore a local feast or festival celebrated in your area or county. Ask your parents, grandparents or neighbours about this. Gather photographs of previous festivals and write a description of the events that took place.

Web Watch!
Chinese game: The Red Envelope Game
http://pbskids.org/sagwa/games/countdown/redenvelopes/index_redenvelopes.html

Get your own Chinese name
http://www.mandarintools.com/chinesename.html

Play some Chinese New Year Games
http://www.primarygames.com/holidays/chinese/games.htm

Integration Project

English

Read about Christmas around the world at http://www.rochedalss.qld.edu.au/xmas/world1.htm

Compare the celebration of this holiday in different countries.

Gaeilge

Tarraing dhá phictiúr den fhéile is fearr leat. Cuir isteach cúpla difríocht bheag idir an dá phictiúr. Tá ar dhuine eile sa rang na difríochtaí a aimsiú.

Mathematics

The first tangrams came from Ancient China. To solve some tangram puzzles, visit:

http://pbskids.org/sagwa/games/tangrams/index.html

Drama

Working in groups, create a freeze frame of your favourite celebration. Each group select an image from this celebration and freeze recreating it. The class try to guess which feast you are celebrating.

Let's Celebrate!

Geography

Write your own A to Z of countries around the world.

List one festival that each country celebrates.

Compare your findings with those of your classmates.

Music

Working in small groups, compose a song about one feast or festival celebrated.

You could choose a popular song and write your own words to describe this celebration.

Art

Design your own wrapping paper for a feast or festival.

Use a large sheet of paper and a sponge to create your own print design.

Science

Design a kite to celebrate the Japanese festival of Kodomono-hi.

What materials will you use?

Test out your design to see if your kite will fly successfully.

Rosa Parks: A Woman who Changed History

Rosa Parks was born Rosa Louise McCauley on 4 February 1913. When her parents divorced, Rosa and her younger brother, Sylvester, moved with their mother to Alabama, USA. There, Rosa grew up on a farm with her grandparents. She attended a black-only school for the five months of the year it was open. It was a small building with one room. There were no windows or desks in the room and the pupils had no books.

When she was not in school, Rosa worked hard on the farm. She dropped out of school at the age of 16 to care for her sick grandmother. Later, she looked after her mother. She married Raymond Parks in 1932. In 1933, she returned to school to finish her education. She and her husband settled in Montgomery, Alabama. In 1943, Rosa Parks attempted to register to vote. She was unsuccessful. It was not until her third attempt in 1945 that she was able to register.

Word Watch!
Segregation laws

To segregate means to set apart from the rest. There were many segregation laws. These laws meant that buses, lifts, restaurants and many other public places were set apart for white people and black people. For example, there was one restaurant for white people and another for blacks. There were water fountains for white people only and another set for black people.

Separate, not Equal

In the early 1950s, the bus system in Montgomery was segregated. Two-thirds of the people using the bus in Montgomery were black. Blacks were required to pay their fare to the driver, then get off and re-board through the back door. Sometimes the bus would drive off before customers who had paid made it to the back. Blacks were required to sit at the back of the bus and give up their seat to white passengers if the bus was full.

Children explore the life of Rosa Parks, a woman who played a significant role in the Civil Rights Movement in the USA.

Rosa Parks worked as a seamstress in a Montgomery department store. On 1 December 1955, she was taking a bus home from work. She paid her fare at the front of the bus, stepped off and re-entered at the rear. The bus filled up and the bus driver asked her to give up her seat to a white man. However, Rosa Parks remained in her seat. She quietly refused to give up her seat and was arrested. She was taken to the police station, fingerprinted, photographed and jailed.

My only concern was to get home after a hard day's work!

The only tired I was, was tired of giving up!

I knew someone had to take the first step and I made up my mind not to move.

The action by Rosa Parks not to give up her seat gave black people hope that they could stand up for their civil rights. Word of her arrest spread and people began to protest. This led to a boycott of the bus system in Montgomery. On Monday 5 December, thousands of leaflets were distributed calling for a boycott of city buses. More than 42,000 protestors refused to travel using the buses. They shared cars, cycled or simply walked the long distances to work.

This boycott was extended and lasted for 381 days. It was a success and resulted in the ending of segregation on the buses in Montgomery. Black people were now allowed to sit on any seat on the bus. The action of Rosa Parks had a huge impact on history.

Word Watch!
Boycott
To refuse to have dealings with a person or organisation. The word comes from Captain Boycott (1832–97), an Irish land agent, whose tenants refused to pay rent to him.

POLICE DEPARTMENT
CITY OF MONTGOMERY

Misc

Date 12-1-55 19

Complainant J.F.Blake (wm)

Address 27 No. Lewis St. Phone No.

Offense Misc. Reported By Same as above

Address Phone No.

Date and Time Offense Committed 12-1-55 6:06 pm

Place of Occurrence In Front of Empire Theatre (On Montgomery Street)

Person or Property Attacked

How Attacked

Person Wanted

Value of Property Stolen Value Recovered

Details of Complaint (list, describe and give value of property stolen)

We received a call upon arrival the bus operator said he had a colored female

sitting in the white section of the bus, and would not move back.

We (Day & Mixon) also saw her.

The bus operator signed a warrant for her. Rosa Parks,(cf) 634 Cleveland Court.

Rosa Parks (cf) was charged with chapter 6 section 11 of the Montgomery City Code.

Warrant #14254

THIS OFFENSE IS DECLARED:
UNFOUNDED ☐
CLEARED BY ARREST ☐
EXCEPTIONALLY CLEARED ☐
INACTIVE (NOT CLEARED) ☐

Officers J. D. Day
D. W. Mixon

Division Patrol Time 7:00 pm
12-1-55

Police report about the arrest of Rosa Parks

Study the Police report above and answer the following questions.

1 Who was arrested?
2 Who arrested her?
3 When and where was she arrested?
4 Why was she arrested?
5 What was Rosa Parks' address?
6 Is there any information about the arrest that you would like to know?
7 How, do you think, did Rosa Parks feel when she was arrested?

A young minister, Rev. Martin Luther King Jr, became a spokesperson for the Montgomery bus boycott. He did not agree with violence and he urged people to protest without using force. He was a great speaker and his words helped to convince many people to join the boycott.

> There comes a time that people get tired. We are here this evening to say to those who have mistreated us so long that we are tired – tired of being segregated and humiliated; tired of being kicked about by the brutal feet of oppression... One of the great glories of democracy is the right to protest for right...

Martin Luther King's Boycott Speech

Rosa Parks is an example of how one person can change the course of history. She knew that change was needed and she had the courage to do what was necessary. She stood up for what she believed in and what she thought was right. She is often called the 'Mother of the Civil Rights Movement'. She was tired of being treated as a second-class citizen. Rosa Parks 'sat down' for justice and equality.

Fast Fact!
Rosa Parks' autobiography, *Quiet Strength*, was published in 1994. She died on 24 October 2005, aged 92.

Question Time

1 Describe Rosa Parks' school life.
2 Why did Rosa Parks have to drop out of school?
3 What was Rosa Parks' job when she was arrested?
4 How, do you think, did Rosa Parks feel when she was asked to give up her seat to a white passenger?
5 How long did the Montgomery bus boycott last?
6 Was the boycott a success?
7 Why is Rosa Parks called the 'Mother of the Civil Rights Movement'?

Creative Time

1 Write ten interview questions that you would have liked to ask Rosa Parks about her life.
   Visit: http://teacher.scholastic.com/rosa/interview.htm#brave to read an interview with Rosa Parks. How do your questions compare?
2 Write a script for a role play re-enacting Rosa Parks' historic bus ride.
3 Design your own poster encouraging the people of Montgomery to boycott the buses. Your poster should convince them how important it is not to use the bus.

Bus Boycott!

Don't ride the bus to work, to town, to school, or any place Monday, 5 December... take a cab, or share a ride, or walk.

Puzzle Time

Choose the correct answer:

1 Where was Rosa Parks born?
   (a) New Ross   (b) Alabama   (c) Washington   (d) New York

2 What was Rosa Parks' job?
   (a) Teacher   (b) Doctor   (c) Bus driver   (d) Seamstress

3 What are civil rights?
   (a) Basic human   (b) Right to be   (c) Right to sit   (d) Right to work
       rights that   kind   down
       people have

4 In what year was Rosa Parks arrested?
   (a) 1944   (b) 1954   (c) 1955   (d) 1965

5 How long did the bus boycott last?
   (a) 80 days   (b) 122 days   (c) 381 days   (d) 200 days

6 Who organised the bus boycott?
   (a) Martin Luther   (b) Rosa Parks   (c) Michael King   (d) Jesse James
       King Jr.

Time Detective

Working as an historian, draw a timeline of Rosa Parks' life. Remember to include all the important events in her life.

Integration Project

English

Write a poem about the life and achievements of Rosa Parks.

Include images and events from her life.

Drama

Freeze Frame: Create a freeze frame of the historic moment when Rosa Parks refused to give up her seat on the bus.

Take on the role of different people on that bus and freeze in character.

Share their thoughts.

SPHE

Write about someone who has influenced your life and whom you respect greatly.

Call your story: 'Someone I Admire'.

Gaeilge

Déan agallaimh i mbeirteanna ag cur ceisteanna ar Rosa Parks.

Bíodh duine amháin ina c(h)eisteoir, agus an duine eile mar Rosa Parks.

Rosa Parks

Art

Using chalk or oil pastels, create a portrait of Rosa Parks.

Hang your class portraits together along with some famous quotes from Rosa Parks.

Mathematics

The bus fares for two adults and three children cost €14.
If a child's fare is half of an adult's fare, what is the adult's fare?

Geography

To plan a bus tour of Ireland, visit:

http://www.buseireann.ie/bubble.php?id=58

Include ten bus trips and visit as many counties as possible on your trip. List all the towns and cities you visit. Enjoy!

Science

Learn about some African-American scientists who had to overcome great challenges and prejudices to achieve great things.
Some were born into slavery and were not allowed a formal education.
Visit:

http://www.infoplease.com/spot/bhmscientists1.html

Answer: €4

Martin Luther King was born in Atlanta, USA, on 15 January, 1929. His father was a Baptist minister and his mother was a school teacher. His parents taught him to treat all people with respect.

At a young age, Martin Luther King learned that black people and white people were not treated in the same manner. He had a friend who was a white boy. One day, his friend's parents told him that he was not allowed to play with their son anymore. Martin felt that this was unjust and he could not understand why all people could not be treated in the same way.

Martin was a very good student at school and he began college at the young age of fifteen. He became a minister like his father and grandfather before him. He later went on to qualify with a PhD from Boston University.

While in college, Martin Luther King learned about Mahatmas Gandhi, an important leader in India. He urged people to protest non-violently. King would later follow Gandhi's example.

Fast Facts!

Mahatmas Gandhi was born in India on 2 October 1869. He studied as a barrister in London. In 1893, he moved to South Africa. Here, he witnessed racism at first hand. He was moved from a first-class to a third-class train coach, even though he had bought a first-class ticket.

In 1915, he returned to India. He helped to free the Indian people from British rule in a non-violent way. He dedicated his life to peaceful methods of protest. He was assassinated in 1948.

Children explore the life of Martin Luther King and his contribution to the Civil Rights Movement in the USA.

On 1 December 1955, a black woman named Rosa Parks refused to give up her seat on a bus to a white man. She was arrested and jailed. King organised a successful year-long boycott of the city buses.

During this boycott, King was arrested and jailed. His home was bombed and many threats were made against his life. However, King was not frightened and he later became a respected leader of the Civil Rights Movement.

In 1953, he married Coretta Scott and they had four children. King and his family moved to Atlanta in 1960. He wanted to change the segregation laws that made black people use separate fountains, toilets and restaurants.

For the next twelve years, King led the fight for civil rights in the South. He organised marches and peaceful protests so that black people could have the same rights as white people. He wanted black people to have the right to vote, the right to better education, and the right to better housing.

Ku Klux Klan

The Ku Klux Klan was a group of white people who attacked black people and any white people who supported black people. They wore white sheets and hats. The black community lived in terror because of the violence of the Ku Klux Klan.

Peaceful Protests

In 1960, students who supported the Civil Rights Movement organised sit-ins. Black people would go to coffee shops, restaurants or hotels, and if they were not served, they would sit down and refuse to move. Many of these protesters were beaten by the police and arrested.

Martin Luther King (2nd from left) meets President Kennedy (4th from right)

In 1961, Freedom Rides began in Washington DC. Groups of black and white people travelled on buses together around the South to challenge segregation. The buses were attacked and stoned. One black Freedom Rider was covered with petrol and set alight. When pictures of these scenes were broadcast on national TV, the Civil Rights Movement became headline news. In September 1961, the law was changed and black people were given equal rights to sit where they wanted to on the buses.

In 1962, King met with John F. Kennedy to talk to him about the Civil Rights Movement. The meeting between King and Kennedy was very important. For King, it gave a new status to the Civil Rights Movement.

In June 1963, Kennedy addressed the American people and he said:

My fellow Americans, this is a problem which faces us all. . . . We cannot say to ten per cent of the population that you can't have that right; that your children can't have the chance to develop whatever talents they have; that the only way that they are going to get their rights is to go into the streets and demonstrate. I think we owe them and we owe ourselves a better country than that. Therefore, I am asking for your help in making it easier for us to move ahead and to provide the kind of equality of treatment which we would want ourselves; to give a chance for every child to be educated to the limit of his talents.

I Have a Dream

In August 1963, King delivered his famous 'I have a dream' address at a march in Washington DC. 250,000 supporters attended the march and listened to King's powerful speech.

> I have a dream that my four little children will one day live in a nation where they will not be judged by the colour of their skin but by the content of their character. I have a dream today... I have a dream that one day... little black boys and black girls will be able to join hands with little white boys and white girls and walk together as sisters and brothers.

In December 1964, Martin Luther King was awarded a Nobel Peace Prize for his work as a leader of the Civil Rights Movement.

A Great Leader

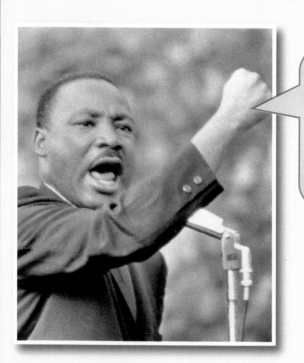

I've been to the mountain top and seen the Promised Land. I may not get there with you. But I want you to know tonight that we, as a people, will get to the Promised Land.

3 April 1968

Web Watch!

You can read the full speech on this website: http://www.afscme.org/about/1549.cfm

On 3 April 1968, King spoke at a march in Memphis, Tennessee. The following day, he was assassinated while standing on the balcony of his hotel room. He was only 39 years old.

Martin Luther King was one of America's greatest leaders. The third Monday in January is celebrated as a national holiday in America. This marks the great work he did throughout his life.

President Barack Obama

Barack Obama was born in Hawaii in 1961. His father was from Kenya. His mother was from Kansas and of Irish descent. He worked as Director of Community Projects and later attended Harvard Law School.

Barack Obama is the first black American President. On 20 January 2009, he took office as America's forty-fourth president. In his victory speech to thousands of Americans, Obama stated that 'change has come to America'.

Martin Luther King had dreamt of this change.

President Barack Obama

Question Time

1 Where was Martin Luther King born? *atlanta*
2 What was his profession? *civil rights activist*
3 Who inspired and influenced Martin Luther King? *muohdtamavhm ghandi*
4 What was the famous speech Dr King gave in Washington DC called? *i have a dream*
5 Describe some of the peaceful protests carried out. *sit in*
6 What great honour did Dr King receive in 1964? *peace prize*
7 How did Martin Luther King die? *assassination*
8 Why, do you think, is Martin Luther King Day in January? *He was born in Tenva*

Creative Time

1 Read the full text of Martin Luther King's famous 'I have a dream' speech
 on: http://news.bbc.co.uk/2/hi/americas/3170387.stm
 Write your own speech about your dreams for a better world.
2 Design your own stamp commemorating the life of Martin Luther King.
3 Write an acrostic poem about Martin Luther King's life. Each line should
 begin with a different letter of his name.

M _____
A _____
R _____
T _____
I _____
N _____

L _____
U _____
T _____
H _____
E _____
R _____

K _____
I _____
N _____
G _____

Puzzle Time

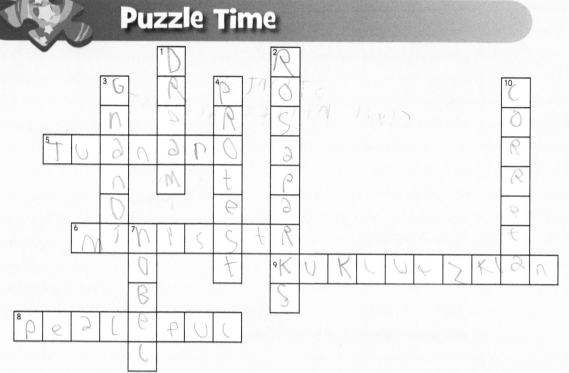

The crossword answers (handwritten):

- **5 Across:** JANUARY
- **6 Across:** MINISTER
- **8 Across:** PEACEFUL
- **9 Across:** KU KLUX KLAN
- **1 Down:** DREAM
- **2 Down:** ROSA PARKS
- **3 Down:** GANDHI
- **4 Down:** PROTEST
- **7 Down:** NOBEL
- **10 Down:** CORRETTE

Across

5 Martin Luther King Day is celebrated in this month.

6 Martin Luther King was a Baptist _____

8 The type of protests organised by Martin Luther King.

9 The group of white people that terrorised black people. (3 words)

Down

1 Dr. King's famous speech, 'I have a _____'

2 This brave woman refused to give up her seat to a white man on a bus. (2 words)

3 Dr. King was influenced by this important leader in India.

4 King organised a year-long _____ of the city buses.

7 Martin Luther King was awarded the _____ Peace Prize in 1964.

10 Martin Luther King's wife.

Time Detective

1 Fill in the dates and the blanks on the timeline of Martin Luther King's life.

King marries
Connetta Scott

'I have a Dream'

King is born in atlanta

Bus boycott in 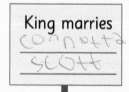 Washington

Assassinated in 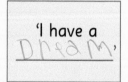 1968

2 Research other winners of the Nobel Peace Prize. Find out about their lives and contribution to peace.

Integration Project

English

Imagine that you were a member of the crowd on the day that Martin Luther King gave his historic 'I have a dream' speech. How did you feel while you listened to him? Were you moved by his speech?

Gaeilge

Déan póstaer bunaithe ar an téama 'Síocháin'.

Cuir isteach pictiúir agus focail bunaithe ar an téama.

Mathematics

Take the Martin Luther King quiz at:

http://seattletimes.nwsource.com/special/mlk/classroom/MLKquiz.html

What was your score as a percentage? What was the highest score in the class? What was the average score?

Drama

Working in small groups, write a short play based on one event in the life of Martin Luther King. You could act out this event for your classmates.

Martin Luther King

Geography

On a blank map of America, mark in the important places in the life of King such as Atlanta, Boston, Washington DC, Montgomery and Memphis.

Science

King was awarded the Nobel Peace Prize for his role in leading non-violent Civil Rights protests.

Investigate the inventor Alfred Nobel after whom this award was named.

Music

Listen to and discuss the words of the Civil Rights song *We Shall Overcome*.
Visit:

http://www.k-state.edu/english/nelp/american.studies.s98/we.shall.overcome.html

SPHE

Divide the class in half. Half the class wear green badges, the other half wear purple badges.
At break time, you are allowed to play only with those wearing the same colour badge as you. Those wearing purple badges are allowed in one area of the yard only.
Discuss how you felt.

Throughout history, there have been remarkable women who have overcome great obstacles to achieve their goals. It was difficult for women to achieve success in the past. They had to fight to get equal rights, rights to the same jobs as men. They even had to fight for the right to vote.

Great Firsts

First Doctor
The Egyptian Merit Ptah is thought to be the first female doctor.

First Vote
New Zealand was the first country to grant all women the right to vote.

2700 BC

1893

42 BC

1903

First Protester
Hortensia was the first woman to lead a march for women's rights, protesting against the unfair taxes on women.

First Nobel Prize
Marie Curie was the first woman to receive a Nobel Prize for physics, for the discovery of radium.

First female Member of Parliament in Ireland

In 1918, Countess Markievicz was elected the first female Member of Parliament in Ireland.

First Irish President

Mary Robinson was elected the first female President of Ireland.

First Prime Minister

Sirimavo Bandaranaike from Ceylon, now Sri Lanka, was elected Prime Minister on 20 July, 1960. She became the first female Prime Minister in the world.

1918   **1960**   **1990**

1932

1963

First Solo Flight

Amelia Earhart was the first woman to fly solo across the Atlantic Ocean.

World Leaders

In the past, there have been many women rulers such as Queen Elizabeth of England in the 16th century, Catherine the Great of Russia in the 18th century, and Queen Victoria of England in the 19th century. In modern times, women such as Margaret Thatcher, Benazir Bhutto and Indira Gandhi have been Prime Ministers in their countries.

1   Investigate how many world leaders today are women.
2   How does this compare to men? Why, do you think, is this so?

First Woman in Space

The Russian cosmonaut Valentina Tereshkova was the first woman in space, spending three days orbiting the Earth.

Women Who Made a Difference

Sojourner Truth (1797-1883)

Sojourner Truth was born a slave in New York. After she was freed, she set out as a travelling preacher. She spoke out against slavery and for the rights of women. She helped newly freed slaves.

Florence Nightingale (1820-1910)

Florence Nightingale worked as a nurse during the Crimean War. She worked 20-hour days and she inspired other nurses to improve the medical system in hospitals. They helped to reduce the death rate from 42 per cent to just 2 per cent. After the war, she founded a school for nurses in London.

Harriet Tubman (1820-1913)

Harriet Tubman was born a slave in Maryland, USA. She risked her life to lead slaves to freedom. She saved as many as 300 slaves and was known as 'the Moses of her people', after Moses in the Bible.

Mother Teresa (1910-1997)

Mother Teresa was a nun who went to work in India. She was famous for nursing the sick and teaching the poor. She received the Nobel Peace Prize for her work in Calcutta, India.

Right to Vote

In most countries, women did not have the right to vote until the 20th century. Through determination and perseverance, women finally got the vote. Suffragettes were brave and courageous women who were dedicated to getting women the vote. They carried out direct action such as chaining themselves to railings, smashing windows, heckling at public meetings and going on hunger strike. One suffragette, Emily Davison, died after she stepped out in front of the King's horse at the Epsom Derby in 1913.

Emmeline Pankhurst (1857-1928)

Emmeline Pankhurst and her daughter, Christabel, led the Suffragettes in Britain in the early 1900s. At first they organised peaceful marches and demonstrations. These actions did not work so they turned to more extreme methods. They were willing to break the law in order to get the right to vote. Emmeline was arrested many times. In prison, she went on hunger strike but she was forced to eat food against her will.

When World War I broke out in 1914, suffragettes encouraged women to help with the war, doing the jobs that the men used to do. This helped to persuade the British government to grant women the vote.

Emmeline Pankhurst carried away by a policeman

Timeline of when women got the vote

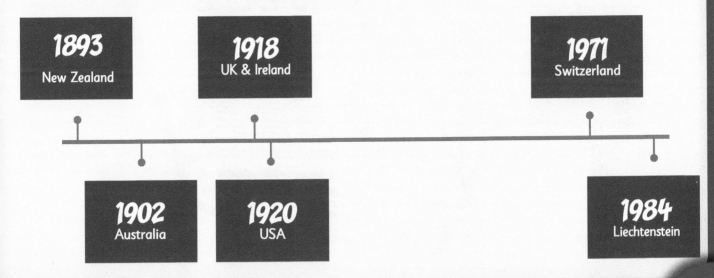

1893 New Zealand

1918 UK & Ireland

1971 Switzerland

1902 Australia

1920 USA

1984 Liechtenstein

 **Question Time**

1 What was Marie Curie's great accomplishment?
2 Who was the first woman in space?
3 Name the first female president of Ireland.
4 What difference did Florence Nightingale make?
5 Why, do you think, was Harriet Tubman named 'the Moses of her people'?
6 Who were the suffragettes?
7 Why did their protest turn more extreme?
8 What was the first country to grant women the right to vote?
9 In what year did Ireland give women the right to vote?
10 Why, do you think, were Irish women not given the vote earlier?

 **Creative Time**

1 Create your own coin honouring a woman who accomplished great things. Design the front and back of your coin. Put some suitable words or phrase on your coin.
2 Compose your own song called 'Women Who Dare!' You could use a popular song and rewrite the lyrics, or make up a rap song.
3 Write a newspaper article about one woman who made a difference. Tell about what she achieved and the influence she has had on women's rights.

Puzzle Time

1 Match these women to their photographs.

Oprah Winfrey
Hilary Clinton
Marie Curie
Amelia Earhart
Rosa Parks
Mother Teresa

2 Find the names of these women in the wordsearch.

- Amelia Earhart
- Hortensia
- Marie Curie
- Mary Robinson
- Mother Teresa
- Rosa Parks
- Sojourner Truth

```
C U O U N R N S N Y Y E D K I
U D U G W E S H O G E S Y R H
L M V K I Q W U U O E D B V L O
L M O T H E R T E R E S A I U R
V O I M A R I E C U Y R I E W T
J N O S N I B O R Y R R A M B E
F B W B S Q K R O E T Q R Z N
H T U R T R E N R U O J O S S
P A M E L I A E A R D H A R T I
R H C J R R W X Y D I M W V A
C W P K J U F T L R U J W N T
C J R H G M C R I L S M U B Q
J H K Y K C C Y C V O X O E V Y
U A I S N E T R O H J K T V Y
W I R H C X S K R A P A S O R
```

Time Detective

Encyclopaedia
of
Great Women

Your class are going to produce an *Encyclopaedia of Great Women*. First, brainstorm about all the women who have achieved great things. Then, arrange them into different categories:

- Women and Science
- Women and Politics
- Women and Sports
- Women and the Arts
- Women who made a difference.

Make sure to include women from many different groups. Each person in your class chooses one great woman. Research your chosen person. Prepare a one-page report outlining her background, education and achievements. Include a photograph, or a drawing of the woman. All the reports can be put together to make a class *Encyclopaedia of Great Women*.

Web Watch!

http://www.kidspoint.org/columns2.asp?column_id=1252&column_type=homework

Integration Project

English

Create a class notice board of your favourite quotes from famous women.

See some quotations on:
http://memory.loc.gov/learn/features/womenswords/

Gaeilge

Fiche Ceist: Smaoiníonn páiste amháin ar bhean ar fhoglainn sibh fúithi.

Cuireann na páistí fiche ceist air/uirthi chun an bhean a thomhas.

Mathematics

To learn about women mathematicians in the past and their achievements, visit:

http://www.agnesscott.edu/lriddle/women/chronol.htm

Drama

A right is a privilege a person is guaranteed by law.

Organise a class debate about rights that you think women should have but have not yet achieved.

Women Who Dare!

Geography

Investigate great female explorers at:

http://www.enchantedlearning.com/explorers/women.shtml

SPHE

Create a 'Women's Hall of Fame' in your school featuring women in your community or county.

Research local newspapers and magazines.

Art

Design your own poster on 'Women, Then and Now'.

Include information about how women's lives have changed over the years and some interesting historic facts about women.

Science

To learn about some amazing women's adventures in science, visit:

http://www.iwaswondering.org/index2.html?gclid=CMncnt6OtZYCFQpPQgodUEQhLQ

Now, it is quiz time. Your class can answer the quiz in small groups of four, or write the answers by yourself.

Round One: Story

1 Why was Rosa Parks arrested?
2 What was Rosa Parks' job when arrested?
3 What were segregation laws?
4 What is a boycott?
5 Why is Rosa Parks called the 'Mother of the Civil Rights Movement'?
6 What was Martin Luther King's profession?
7 Who inspired Martin Luther King?
8 What was the famous speech Dr King gave in Washington DC called?
9 What great honour did Dr King receive in 1964?
10 How did Martin Luther King die?

Round Two: Early Civilisations

1 Where did the Aztecs come from originally?
2 Why did they build their city in the middle of a lake?
3 What were *chinampas*?
4 Name the most important Aztec god.
5 Name the Spanish explorer who landed in the Aztec Empire in 1519.
6 What was the capital of the Kingdom of Benin?
7 What were the people of the Kingdom of Benin called?
8 What was the king called?
9 Where is the Kingdom of Benin located?
10 What were a group of craftspeople called?

Children revise and consolidate information they have learned.

Round Three: Placenames and Festivals

1. What does a placename beginning with 'Cill' mean?
2. What does a placename containing 'Rath' tell you?
3. What does a placename beginning with 'Bally' or 'Ballin' tell you?
4. What is a shallow crossing in a river called?
5. What does a placename beginning with 'Carraig' or 'Carrick' mean?
6. Name three festivals celebrated around the world.
7. When is Independence Day in America?
8. Name a Jewish festival which is celebrated.
9. How is the Chinese New Year celebrated?
10. What Celtic festival did Hallowe'en come from?

Round Four: Famine and 1916

1. When did the Great Famine take place?
2. Why did the Famine occur?
3. What was an absentee landlord?
4. What were soup kitchens?
5. What were coffin ships?
6. Name the different organisations that took part in the 1916 Rising.
7. Where were the rebels' headquarters?
8. Name some of the buildings taken over by rebels.
9. What was O'Connell Street called in 1916?
10. How long did the 1916 Rising last?

Round Five: Explorers and Revolution

1. What are some of the reasons for exploration?
2. Name the explorer who officially first discovered America.
3. Name two Irish explorers.
4. Which explorer led the first expedition around the world?
5. Name the three ships Columbus used on his expedition.
6. Why was there a revolution in America?
7. What was the motto of the French Revolution?
8. Who were the United Irishmen?
9. When did the Rebellion take place in Ireland?
10. Where did most of the fighting take place?

Round Six: Historic Photographs
Can you name these historic figures?

Score: ____ /56

Chapter	Topic	Website reference
1	Buildings and Ruins in my Area	http://www.irishtimes.com/ancestor/placenames/ http://goireland.about.com/od/historyculture/qt/irishplacenames.htm www.of-ireland.info/castle.html http://www.buildingsofireland.ie/Surveys/Buildings/
2	Let's Communicate!	http://www.battleshipnc.com/kids/games/morse/index.php http://www.telephonymuseum.com/telephone%20history.htm http://www.computersciencelab.com/ComputerHistory/History.htm
3	Explorers Over Time	http://www.patfalvey.com http://www.kidinfo.com/American_History/Explorers.html http://www.famousexplorers.net/
4	The Aztecs	http://www.innovationslearning.co.uk/subjects/history/information/aztecs/aztecs_home.htm http://library.thinkquest.org/4034/cortes.html http://home.freeuk.net/elloughton13/aztecs.htm
5	The Kingdom of Benin	http://africa.mrdonn.org/benin.html http://www.hamillgallery.com/BENIN/BeninArt.html http://www.dia.org/collections/aonwc/africanart/beninkings.html
6	Revolution and Change	http://www.teachnet.ie/jheffernan/2006/Page3.htm http://www.nationalarchives.ie/PDF/1798.pdf . http://www.iol.ie/~98com/ballads.htm
7	An Gorta Mór	http://www.historyplace.com/worldhistory/famine/introduction.htm http://www.limerick.com/lifestyle/soupkitchen.html http://www.techlearning.com/webpicks/showArticle.php?articleID=192202601 http://school.discoveryeducation.com/lessonplans/programs/forcedtoflee/
8	Irish Cultural Revival	http://www.gaa.ie http://multitext.ucc.ie/d/Ireland_religion__culture_1870-1914 http://www.cnag.ie/
9	Easter Rising 1916	http://www.taoiseach.gov.ie/eng/index.asp?docID=2518 http://www.irishtimes.com/focus/easterrising/ http://www.nli.ie/1916/1916_main.html
10	Let's Celebrate!	http://www.festivals.com/ http://hgpho.to/wfest/flower/flower-e.html http://www.chinapage.com/festival/festival.html http://www.woodlands-junior.kent.sch.uk/Homework/religion/calendar.htm
11	Rosa Parks	http://www.rosaparks.org/bio.html http://teacher.scholastic.com/ROSA/interview.htm http://www.kidspoint.org/columns2.asp?column_id=1252&column_type=homework http://www.travellady.com/Issues/September03/RosaParksMuseum.htm
12	Martin Luther King	http://www.bbc.co.uk/history/historic_figures/gandhi_mohandas.shtml http://library.thinkquest.org/J0112391/freedom_rides.htm http://news.bbc.co.uk/2/hi/americas/3170387.stm
13	Women Who Dare!	http://teacher.scholastic.com/activities/women/ http://www.cam-info.net/femhist.html http://www.pocanticohills.org/womenenc/womenenc.htm

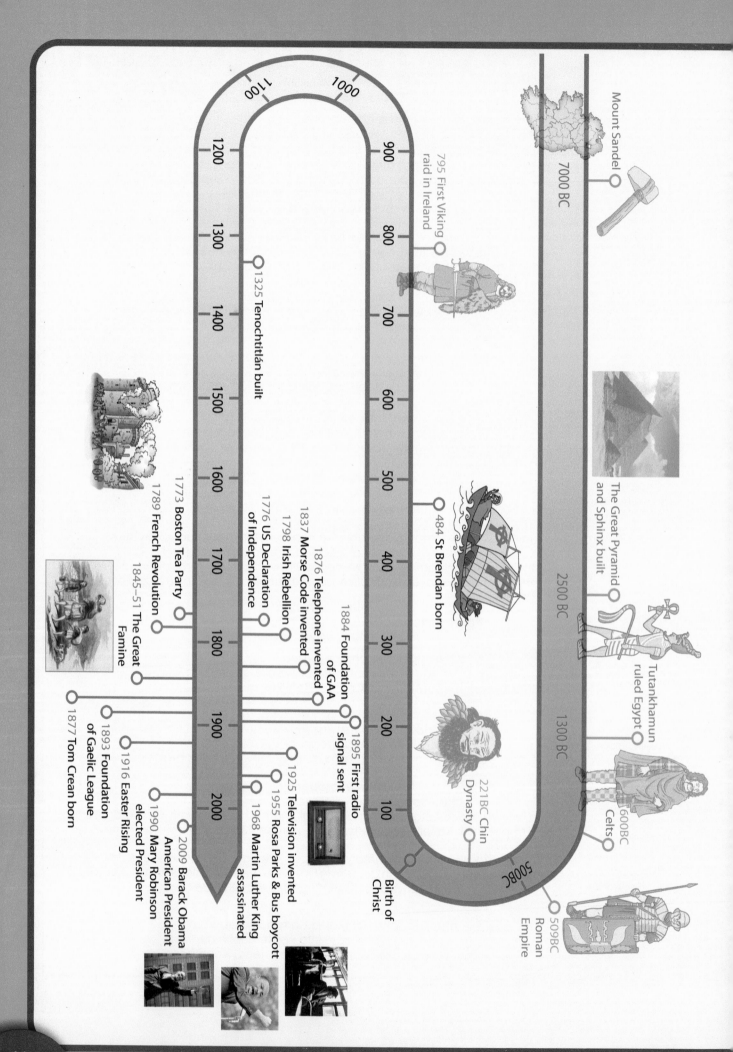

Mount Sandel

7000 BC

2500 BC The Great Pyramid and Sphinx built

1300 BC Tutankhamun ruled Egypt

600BC Celts

509BC Roman Empire

500BC

221BC Chin Dynasty

Birth of Christ

100

200

300

400

484 St Brendan born

500

600

700

795 First Viking raid in Ireland

800

900

1000

1100

1200

1300

1325 Tenochtitlán built

1400

1500

1600

1700

1773 Boston Tea Party

1776 US Declaration of Independence

1789 French Revolution

1798 Irish Rebellion

1800

1837 Morse Code invented

1845–51 The Great Famine

1876 Telephone invented

1877 Tom Crean born

1884 Foundation of GAA

1893 Foundation of Gaelic League

1895 First radio signal sent

1900

1916 Easter Rising

1925 Television invented

1955 Rosa Parks & Bus boycott

1968 Martin Luther King assassinated

1990 Mary Robinson elected President

2000

2009 Barack Obama American President